Mostly Fluency...

Five Minutes to Fluency and Comprehension Level I

Whole Class or One-on-One

Intervention Made Easy

© 2015 Lucky Willy Publishing and imprint of Lucky Jenny Publishing Inc., Plymouth, California. All rights reserved. Academic duplication for one classroom is authorized. Contact publisher@luckyjenny.com for extended permissions.

ISBN 978-0692503782

Table of Contents

Instructions for Fluency Letter Pages	5
Instructions for Fluency Practice for a Group or Class	6
A Few Words About Reading Instruction	9
Practice Passages: Letters to Words	11
Short "a" Letter Page	12
Short "e" Letter Page	14
Short "i" Letter Page	16
Short "o" Letter Page	18
Short "u" Letter Page	20
Long "a" Letter Page	22
Long "e" Letter Page	24
Long "i" Letter Page	26
Long "o" Letter Page	28
Long "u" Letter Page	30
"c" Letter Page	32
"m" Letter Page	34
"p" Letter Page	36
"f" Letter Page	38
"b" Letter Page	40
"ar" Letter Page	42
"ar" and "ur" Letter Page	44
"ow" Letter Page	46
Passages	**49**
High Frequency Words	50
Fluency "ir", "or" and "our"	56
Fluency Words "long e spelled y"	58
Fluency Words "Contractions"	61
Fluency Words "Consonant Pairs"	64
Fluency "th" Words	67
Fluency "s" or "es" Words	70
Fluency Soft "c" and "s" Words	73
Fluency Words "Compound Words"	76
Fluency Words "f", "ff" and "ough"	79
Fluency Words "w", "wh" and "h"	82
Fluency Words "More High Frequency Words"	85
Fluency Words "Even More HFW"	88
Fluency "Words, Words, Words"	91
Fluency "Words Again"	94
Fluency "Words Revisited"	97
Fluency "More Words to Read	100
Fluency "The Other Sound of C	103
Fluency "Almost Last Set of Words"	106
Fluency "Last Set of Words"	109
Fluency "Action Words"	112
Fluency "Things"	113
Fluency D, F and G Words	114
Words to Read and Know	**115**
Fluency First Hundred	116
Fluency First Hundred – Part 2	117
Fluency First Hundred – Part 3	118
Vowels	**119**
Fluency Short Vowels "a"	121
Fluency Short Vowels "e"	123
Fluency Short Vowel "I"	125
Fluency Short Vowel "o"	127
Fluency Short Vowel "u"	129
Fluency Long Vowels "a"	131
Fluency Long "e"	133
Fluency Long "I"	135
Fluency Long "o" Words	137
Fluency Long "u" Words	139
Passages	**141**
Story Passages	**179**
Inventory Sheets and Logs	**191**

Instruction for Fluency Letter Pages

For very early readers - the letter fluency pages are intended to be guided. For struggling students or those who just need more practice – follow whole group instructions.

Working One on One: Point to the first letter and say the letter sound. Point to the second letter and say the letter sound. Repeat for each letter sound. Point to each word and say the word. Say "Your turn. You do what I did." Point to the first letter and say "What does this say?" Point to the second letter and say: "What does this say?" Point to the third letter and say: "What does this say?" Repeat for each letter sound. Point to each word and say: "Read the word." Have reader repeat the whole process until words are easily read. This works with parents, aides and older students as facilitators too!

Working In a Group Setting…

Teacher Say: We are going to do the letter pages together

s	a	t
c	a	t
m	a	t
sat	cat	mat

SAY: /ss/ as you *point to the first letter sound.*

SAY: /a/ as you *point to the second letter sound.*

Repeat for each letter sound.
Next, point to each word and say the word.

Say: sat *(pause)* cat *(pause)* mat *(pause)*

Say: "Your turn. You do what I did."

Say: "What does this say?" *Point to the first letter.*
Say: "What does this say?" *Point to the second letter.*
Say: "What does this say?" *Point to the third letter.*

Repeat for each letter sound.

Point to each word and **Say:** "Read the word."

Have group/class repeat the whole process until words are easily read

Instruction for Fluency Practice For a Group or a Whole Class

Increasing student fluency proficiency through word practice and literature is an engaging way to help students move from dragging themselves across endless pages of text – to truly enjoying the written word. The following techniques, designed to move students to reading fluency, are research-based and use highly-effective instructional strategies.

If this manual, or the exercises herein, are being used by parents…please follow the instructions below with the following modification: you are both the teacher and the partner reader, so it may be helpful to have two copies of the same page. If copies are not possible, simply sit across from student and keep track of mistakes on a separate piece of paper. Mark mistakes only when student is finished with the entire reading selection.

Materials:
- One timer
- Two copies of each passage (in sheet protectors to reuse!)
- Two copies of the CP Fluency Record Sheet (kept in folders if each student does not have a book)
- Overhead sheet of: Total Words Read: _____
  Minus errors: _____
  = WPM _____

Instructions for Class Setting

Before you begin, have a copy of one of the Practice Passages on a transparency or display it to the whole class on a document camera, Smartboard, or overhead projector. As you explain the lessons, demonstrate what students will be doing.

Say: We are going to do timed fluency reading in pairs. Fluency is the rate and ease at which we read. The flow of reading. This activity will take about ten minutes and will help us all learn to read more fluently…to help your reading flow smoothly. To practice fluency we are going to read a short passage, figure out how many words we are each reading per minute and then answer some questions about what we have just read. I will read each passage first and then you and your partner will each take turns reading the passage aloud softly and then calculating your words per minute score.

Break students into pairs and hand out one copy per student. If you are working with a group of students with varying abilities it is helpful to pair stronger readers with weaker ones and then assign the stronger reader to read first. Modify the script accordingly.

Say: I am going to demonstrate what you will be doing. *(choose a student to be your "checker")*. Marissa and I are going to demonstrate. Marissa is going to be my "checker". She is going to follow along and put a line over each word I get wrong.

(Practice reading in a normal voice just above a whisper) I am reading in a hushed voice.

Say: Again, while your partner is reading, you will follow along and put a line over each word they read incorrectly. When the timer goes off, you will circle the last word your partner read.

Pause.

Say: What will you do when the timer goes off, everybody *(signal and students should respond: circle the last word your partner read).* **Skip this if you are going to calculate the CWPM** Then you will figure your partner's combined words per minute, or cwpm, score. What will you calculate, everyone *(signal and students should respond: your partner's combined words per minute score).*

Say: Next, you will tell your partner how many words he/she read. You will say: "You read _____ words". What will you say, everyone: *(You will read _____ words.)*

Mark the number of words read on the first line of your DISPLAY copy.

Say: Next, you will say "I heard _____ errors." What will you say, everyone *(I heard _____ errors.)* There will be no arguments about errors. You will not be marked down for the number of errors. You will get credit for doing the assignment.

Mark the number of errors on the second line of your overhead sheet.

Say: Now, you subtract line two ____ from line one _____ to get _____. _____ is the number of correct words.

Pause. If you feel calculating the CWPM is too difficult, just have students mark the total number of errors and calculate the CWPM at a later time.

Select a practice passage.

Say: Since you need to be marking your partner's paper, switch papers now. *(pause)* Now we are going to practice the entire exercise. I am going to read Passage ___ while you follow along. Put your finger on the first word in the box. That word is ____. **(Check to make sure each person is in the right spot and then read the passage).**

Say: Now it is your turn. Raise your hand if you are Partner 1. (**Pause** *until one student from each pair has his/her hand raised.)* Good. Raise your hand if you are Partner 2. (**Pause** *until one student from each pair has his/her hand raised.)* Excellent. When I say "Begin", all Partner 1s should quietly begin to read to their partners. All Partner 2s will use their pencils to keep track of their partner's errors. Partner 2s will put a line over each word pronounced incorrectly. When the timer goes off, all Partner 2s will circle the last word read, but Partner 1s will keep reading until the passage is complete. Does anyone have any questions?

Say: Please get ready **(pause)**. Begin.

When the timer goes off…

Say: Partner 2s, please mark your partner's score and give feedback to Partner 1s.

Walk around the room to make sure scores are being marked accurately and students are being polite.

Say: Now we are going to switch jobs…Partner 2s please get ready to read. Partner 1s please get ready to score. **(Pause and only begin when all students are ready.)**

Say: Begin.

Say: Partner 1s, please mark your partner's score and give feedback to Partner 2s.

Walk around the room to make sure scores are being marked accurately and students are being polite.

Practice this way as many days as required until all of the students understand the process.

NOTE:
- This is a quick and effective way to get RTI fluency practice into a busy day. Keep careful track of your record sheets for evidence. It only takes one or two practices for students to get the hang of this process and then it flows easily and will take no more than five to ten minutes per session.

SUGGESTIONS: Practice fluency at the end of each reading period, at the beginning of each day…or my favorite…right after recess. All readers benefit from fluency practice, so get everyone involved.

A Few Words about Reading Instruction

Effective reading instruction, especially for struggling readers, must be explicit and targeted. Struggling readers are often easily confused and this confusion can lead to frustration. Struggling readers need to be explicitly, or directly, taught the skills they need to be proficient readers.

When teachers instruct explicitly, students don't have to guess what they need to know. They are told outright. In order for reading instruction to be effective, teachers must clearly state the objective, or what the student is supposed to know, when the lesson is complete, demonstrate these skills and clearly explain every concept and nuance.

For example, when using the lessons in this book, when the letter combination /ar/ is taught – the combination must be explained. Before reading the word list say: "The sound these letters make together is "are" – like a pirate says "arrrrr". What does /ar/ say?" Point to the letter combination and let the student repeat.

Say: "When you see /ar/ together, like in the word "card" it will usually say "are"." Then go into the words and passages.

Providing specific feedback and praise is also essential. Research indicates, providing positive guiding feedback is much more effective than criticism. Effective teachers find ways to consistently and consistently provide authentic feedback. Don't say, "good job", but rather, "You figured out how to read "card" all by yourself" or "When you were reading the passage, you corrected your own mistake! Excellent".

Students need information about their errors as well, but simply saying "that was incorrect" is not helpful. Corrective feedback should be similar to the following:
- **"That was so close. This word is *helpful*."**
- **"You made a small mistake in the last sentence. Can you find it?"**
- **"That was so close to being right. Let's try again."**

According to the latest National Report Card for Reading, 67% of fourth graders read below grade level. Readers struggle for various reasons, but research has consistently demonstrated that even when a student is diagnosed with a severe reading disability, factors related to early reading instruction play a big role in determining which students will become struggling readers.

High quality, intensive instruction, and its ability to compensate for neurological and genetic factors, is underestimated (Floorman, Fletcher, and Francis, 1997; Shaywitz, 2003). Studies of brain function shows students with serious reading disabilities can be helped by intensive intervention and said brain function can actually improve. Basically…instruction has the power to change the way a person's brain works. This research is facinating and can easily be found on the internet – just search for: Simos, Breier, Fletcher, Bergman and Floorman.

Final note…it is imperative to fix struggling reading early. A child who is a poor reader by the end of third grade has a 75% chance of being a poor reader by the end of high school.

As we understand more about reading, we get closer and closer to helping every child toward proficient reading.

Practice Passages
Letters to Words

Name: _____ Date: _____

Fluency Letter Page – short "a"

Point to the first letter and say the letter sound. Point to the second letter and say the letter sound. Repeat for each letter sound. Point to each word and say the word. Say "Your turn. You do what I did." Point to the first letter and say: "What does this say?" Point to the second letter and say: "What does this say?" Point to the third letter and say: "What does this say?" Repeat for each letter sound. Point to each word and say: "Read the word." Have reader repeat the whole process until words are easily read.

s	a	t
c	a	t
m	a	t
sat	cat	mat

Notes:

Name: _____ Date: _____

Fluency – short "a"

Read the passage. Say: "Now it is your turn to read the passage."

The cat sat on the mat.

The cat sat on the mat.

cat		sat		mat

The cat sat on the mat.

The cat sat on the mat.

cat		sat		mat

The cat sat on the mat.

The cat sat on the mat.

Notes:

Name: _____ Date: _____

Fluency Letter Page – short "e"

Point to the first letter and say the letter sound, point to the second letter and say the letter sound, point to the third letter and say the letter sound. Point to the word and say the word. Say "Your turn. You do what I did." Point to the first letter and say: "What does this say?" Point to the second letter and say: "What does this say?" Point to the third letter and say: "What does this say?" Point to the words and say: "Read the word." Repeat the whole process, but do so silently – using only hand gestures.

m	e	n
d	e	n
w	e n	t
men	den	went

Notes:

14

Name: _____ Date: _____

Fluency – short "e"

Read the passage aloud. Say: "Now it is your turn to read the passage."

The men went into the den.

The men went into the den.

men　　　went　　　　den

The men went into the den.

The men went into the den.

men　　　went　　　　den

The men went into the den.

The men went into the den.

men　　　went　　　　den

Notes:

Name: _____   Date: _____

Fluency Letter Page – "short i"

Point to the first letter and say the letter sound. Point to the second letter and say the letter sound. Repeat for each letter sound. Point to each word and say the word. Say "Your turn. You do what I did." Point to the first letter and say "What does this say?" Point to the second letter and say: "What does this say?" Point to the third letter and say: "What does this say?" Repeat for each letter sound. Point to each word and say: "Read the word." Have reader repeat the whole process until words are easily read.

i	n	k	ink
b	i	t	bit
h	i	t	hit
w	i	t h	with
t	h	i s	this
l	i	v e s	lives

Notes:

Name: _____ Date: _____

Fluency – "short i"

Read the passage aloud. Say: "Now it is your turn to read the passage."

The pen had blue ink.

Pam bit the apple.

The pig hit the ball.

Come with me to the park.

This is the way to the park.

The pig lives in the barn.

This pen has blue ink.

He lives with his family.

Notes:

Name: _____ Date: _____

Fluency Letter Page – "short o"

Point to the first letter and say the letter sound. Point to the second letter and say the letter sound. Repeat for each letter sound. Point to each word and say the word. Say "Your turn. You do what I did." Point to the first letter and say "What does this say?" Point to the second letter and say: "What does this say?" Point to the third letter and say: "What does this say?" Repeat for each letter sound. Point to each word and say: "Read the word." Have reader repeat the whole process until words are easily read.

o	f	f	off
g	o	t	got
h	o	p	hop
b	o	x	box
p	o	t	pot
n	o	t	not

Notes:

Name: _____ Date: _____

Fluency – "short o"

Read the passage aloud. Say: "Now it is your turn to read the passage."

Pam took off her hat.

She got off the bus.

Hop up on the chair.

The box fell off the chair.

The pot was bubbling over.

Do not sit on top of the table.

He got to the top of the hill.

I am not going to take it off.

Notes:

Name: _____ Date: _____

Fluency Letter Page – "short u"

Point to the first letter and say the letter sound. Point to the second letter and say the letter sound. Repeat for each letter sound. Point to each word and say the word. Say "Your turn. You do what I did." Point to the first letter and say: "What does this say?" Point to the second letter and say: "What does this say?" Point to the third letter and say: "What does this say?" Repeat for each letter sound. Point to each word and say: "Read the word." Have reader repeat the whole process until words are easily read.

t	u	g		tug
b	u	g		bug
h	u	t		hut
m	u	t	t	mutt
p	u	p		pup
	u	p		up

Notes:

Name: _____ Date: _____

Fluency – "short u"

Read the passage aloud. Say: "Now it is your turn to read the passage."

Umbrellas go up.

Tug on the string.

The bug was under the bed.

The mutt was a happy puppy.

The pup was a mutt.

The pup played up in my room.

The pup ate the bug.

Eat up all of the mush.

Notes:

Name: _____ Date: _____

Fluency Letter Page – "long a"

Point to the first letter and say the letter sound. Point to the second letter and say the letter sound. Repeat for each letter sound. Point to each word and say the word. Say "Your turn. You do what I did." Point to the first letter and say: "What does this say?" Point to the second letter and say: "What does this say?" Point to the third letter and say: "What does this say?" Repeat for each letter sound. Point to each word and say: "Read the word." Have reader repeat the whole process until words are easily read.

b	a	b	y	baby
l	a	d	y	lady
a	b	l	e	able
b	a	k	e	bake
m	a	k	e	make
t	a	b	l	e	table

Notes:

Name: _____ Date: _____

Fluency – "long a"

Read the passage aloud. Say: "Now it is your turn to read the passage."

Please play with the baby.

The lady played with the baby.

The lady was able to play.

Bake some cookies please.

Please make your bed.

The baby sat on the table.

Don't make the baby mad.

The lady baked a cake.

Notes:

Name: _____ Date: _____

Fluency Letter Page – "long e"

Point to the first letter and say the letter sound. Point to the second letter and say the letter sound. Repeat for each letter sound. Point to each word and say the word. Say "Your turn. You do what I did." Point to the first letter and say: "What does this say?" Point to the second letter and say: "What does this say?" Point to the third letter and say: "What does this say?" Repeat for each letter sound. Point to each word and say: "Read the word." Have reader repeat the whole process until words are easily read.

s	e	e	see
e	a	r	ear
e	a	t	eat
b	e	e	bee
f	e	e	t	feet
t	r	e	e	tree

Notes:

Name: _____ Date: _____

Fluency – "long e"

Read the passage aloud. Say: "Now it is your turn to read the passage."

> See if you can come.
>
> You hear with your ears.
>
> Eat all of the tasty treat.
>
> The bee buzzed Ben's ear.
>
> Ben's feet were bare.
>
> The bee was in the tree.
>
> The bee buzzed the tree.
>
> See the bee in the tree?

Notes:

Name: _____ Date: _____

Fluency Letter Page – "long i"

Point to the first letter and say the letter sound. Point to the second letter and say the letter sound. Repeat for each letter sound. Point to each word and say the word. Say "Your turn. You do what I did." Point to the first letter and say: "What does this say?" Point to the second letter and say: "What does this say?" Point to the third letter and say: "What does this say?" Repeat for each letter sound. Point to each word and say: "Read the word." Have reader repeat the whole process until words are easily read.

i	c	e		ice
n	i	c	e	nice
r	i	c	e	rice
h	i	k	e	hike
b	i	k	e	bike
f	i	v	e	five
l	i	o	n	lion

Notes:

Name: _____ Date: _____

Fluency – "long i"

Read the passage aloud. Say: "Now it is your turn to read the passage."

> The ice was cold.
>
> It is a nice day.
>
> Mike likes white rice.
>
> Mike took a hike in the woods.
>
> Ride your bike on the street.
>
> Five mice ate white rice.
>
> The loin roared loudly.
>
> The lion was not so nice.
>
> Mike rode his bike to school.

Notes:

Name: _____ Date: _____

Fluency Letter Page – "long o"

Point to the first letter and say the letter sound. Point to the second letter and say the letter sound. Repeat for each letter sound. Point to each word and say the word. Say "Your turn. You do what I did." Point to the first letter and say: "What does this say?" Point to the second letter and say: "What does this say?" Point to the third letter and say: "What does this say?" Repeat for each letter sound. Point to each word and say: "Read the word." Have reader repeat the whole process until words are easily read.

o	l	d		old
h	o	l	e	hole
c	o	l	d	cold
s	o	l	d	sold
b	o	l	d	bold
f	o	l	d	fold
r	o	l	l	roll

Notes:

Name: _____ Date: _____

Fluency – "long o"

Read the passage aloud. Say: "Now it is your turn to read the passage."

> My shoes are old.
>
> There is a hole in the shoe.
>
> The cold gets in the hole.
>
> Jeff sold his last candy bar.
>
> The boy was bold and brave.
>
> Fold your paper in fours.
>
> Roll over and stand up.
>
> The boy sold the cold drink.
>
> The bold boy braved the cold.

Notes:

Name: _____ Date: _____

Fluency Letter Page – "long u"

Point to the first letter and say the letter sound. Point to the second letter and say the letter sound. Repeat for each letter sound. Point to each word and say the word. Say "Your turn. You do what I did." Point to the first letter and say: "What does this say?" Point to the second letter and say: "What does this say?" Point to the third letter and say: "What does this say?" Repeat for each letter sound. Point to each word and say: "Read the word." Have reader repeat the whole process until words are easily read.

u	s	e	use
c	u	b	e	cube
t	u	b	e	tube
c	u	t	e	cute
r	u	l	e	rule
h	u	g	e	huge
t	r	u	e	true

Notes:

Name: _____ Date: _____

Fluency – "long u"

Read the passage aloud. Say: "Now it is your turn to read the passage."

Please use the back door.

The box is a cube.

The tube was long and narrow.

The baby was sweet and cute.

All rules must be followed.

The cube was huge and green.

It is too good to be true.

Use the rules please.

Notes:

Name: _____ Date: _____

Fluency Letter Page – "c"

Point to the first letter and say the letter sound. Point to the second letter and say the letter sound. Repeat for each letter sound. Point to each word and say the word. Say "Your turn. You do what I did." Point to the first letter and say: "What does this say?" Point to the second letter and say: "What does this say?" Point to the third letter and say: "What does this say?" Repeat for each letter sound. Point to each word and say: "Read the word." Have reader repeat the whole process until words are easily read.

c	a	t	cat
c	a	n	can
c	a	r	car
c	u	p	cup
c	u	t	cut
c	o	t	cot

Notes:

Name: _____ Date: _____

Fluency – "c"

Read the passage aloud. Say: "Now it is your turn to read the passage."

> The cat sat on the mat.
>
> The cat kicked the can.
>
> The cat sat in the car.
>
> The cup was on the mat.
>
> The cat cut her paw.
>
> The cat sat on the cot.
>
> The cup was full of cold water.
>
> The cat drank from the cup.

Notes:

Name: _____ Date: _____

Fluency Letter Page – "m"

Point to the first letter and say the letter sound. Point to the second letter and say the letter sound. Repeat for each letter sound. Point to each word and say the word. Say "Your turn. You do what I did." Point to the first letter and say: "What does this say?" Point to the second letter and say: "What does this say?" Point to the third letter and say: "What does this say?" Repeat for each letter sound. Point to each word and say: "Read the word." Have reader repeat the whole process until words are easily read.

m	a	t	mat
m	a	n	man
m	a	p	map
m	o	p	mop
m	i	x	mix
m	u	g	mug

Notes:

Name: _____ Date: _____

Fluency – "m"

Read the passage aloud. Say: "Now it is your turn to read the passage."

> The mat was blue.
>
> The man sat on the mat.
>
> The map showed us the way.
>
> The mop was wet.
>
> The man ate the cake mix.
>
> The mug was filled with water.
>
> The man mopped the mat.
>
> The map was blue and green.

Notes:

Name: _____ Date: _____

Fluency Letter Page – "p"

Point to the first letter and say the letter sound. Point to the second letter and say the letter sound. Repeat for each letter sound. Point to each word and say the word. Say "Your turn. You do what I did." Point to the first letter and say: "What does this say?" Point to the second letter and say: "What does this say?" Point to the third letter and say: "What does this say?" Repeat for each letter sound. Point to each word and say: "Read the word." Have reader repeat the whole process until words are easily read.

p	e	t	pet
p	a	n	pan
p	e	p	pep
p	o	p	pop
p	o	t	pot
P	a	m	Pam

First try, teacher guided: _____ correct   date: _____

Second try, student guided: _____ correct   date: _____

Third try, student guided: _____ correct   date: _____

Fourth try, student guided: _____ correct   date: _____

Name: _____ Date: _____

Fluency – "p"

Read the passage aloud. Say: "Now it is your turn to read the passage."

Pam has a pet pig.

Pam put butter in the pan.

Pam was full of pep.

Pam drank pop with her Pop.

The pot was full of water.

Pam's pet pig was full of pep.

The popcorn popped in the pan.

Pam's pet pig played in the park.

Pam put her pig in the barn.

First try, teacher guided:	_____ correct	date: _____
Second try, student guided:	_____ correct	date: _____
Third try, student guided:	_____ correct	date: _____
Fourth try, student guided:	_____ correct	date: _____

Name: _____ Date: _____

Fluency Letter Page – "f"

Point to the first letter and say the letter sound. Point to the second letter and say the letter sound. Repeat for each letter sound. Point to each word and say the word. Say "Your turn. You do what I did." Point to the first letter and say: "What does this say?" Point to the second letter and say: "What does this say?" Point to the third letter and say: "What does this say?" Repeat for each letter sound. Point to each word and say: "Read the word." Have reader repeat the whole process until words are easily read.

f	i	x		fix
f	a	t		fat
f	a	n		fan
f	o	x		fox
f	u	l	l	full
f	a	s	t	fast
f	i	s	t	fist

First try, teacher guided: _____ correct   date: _____

Second try, student guided: _____ correct   date: _____

Third try, student guided: _____ correct   date: _____

Fourth try, student guided: _____ correct   date: _____

Name: _____ Date: _____

Fluency – "f"

Read the passage aloud. Say: "Now it is your turn to read the passage."

Fix the broken door please.

The fat cat sat on the mat.

The football fan wore blue.

The fox found a new home.

The bag was full of candy.

The fox ran fast.

The boy put his fist in the air.

The fox was faster than the cat.

The can hid from the fox.

First try, teacher guided: _____ correct   date: _____

Second try, student guided: _____ correct   date: _____

Third try, student guided: _____ correct   date: _____

Fourth try, student guided: _____ correct   date: _____

Name: _____ Date: _____

Fluency Letter Page – "b"

Point to the first letter and say the letter sound. Point to the second letter and say the letter sound. Repeat for each letter sound. Point to each word and say the word. Say "Your turn. You do what I did." Point to the first letter and say: "What does this say?" Point to the second letter and say: "What does this say?" Point to the third letter and say: "What does this say?" Repeat for each letter sound. Point to each word and say: "Read the word." Have reader repeat the whole process until words are easily read.

b	e	g		beg
b	u	t		but
b	o	x		box
b	i	g		big
b	e	a	r	bear
b	r	i	n g	bring

First try, teacher guided: _____ correct   date: _____

Second try, student guided: _____ correct   date: _____

Third try, student guided: _____ correct   date: _____

Fourth try, student guided: _____ correct   date: _____

Name: _____ Date: _____

Fluency – "b"

Read the passage aloud. Say: "Now it is your turn to read the passage."

Don't beg me to come.

I want to go but can't.

The box was on the mat.

The cat was big and fat.

The bear at the food.

Please bring me an apple.

The bear broke the box.

First try, teacher guided: _____ correct   date: _____

Second try, student guided: _____ correct   date: _____

Third try, student guided: _____ correct   date: _____

Fourth try, student guided: _____ correct   date: _____

Name: _____ Date: _____

Fluency Letter Page – "ar"

Point to the first letter and say the letter sound. Point to the second letter and say the letter sound. Repeat for each letter sound. Point to each word and say the word. Say "Your turn. You do what I did." Point to the first letter and say: "What does this say?" Point to the second letter and say: "What does this say?" Point to the third letter and say: "What does this say?" Repeat for each letter sound. Point to each word and say: "Read the word." Have reader repeat the whole process until words are easily read.

c	a	r	d		card
h	a	r	d		hard
d	a	r	k		dark
a	p	a	r	t	apart
s	t	a	r	t	start
p	a	r	t	y	party

First try, teacher guided: _____ correct   date: _____

Second try, student guided: _____ correct   date: _____

Third try, student guided: _____ correct   date: _____

Fourth try, student guided: _____ correct   date: _____

Name: _____   Date: _____

Fluency – "ar"

Read the passage aloud. Say: "Now it is your turn to read the passage."

Play the top card first.

It is hard to play darts.

It was a dark and stormy night.

The cookie fell apart.

Start at the first space please.

The party ended at 11 o'clock.

We played on the hard rocks.

The party started at 9:15.

His chain fell apart.

First try, teacher guided:	_____ correct	date: _____
Second try, student guided:	_____ correct	date: _____
Third try, student guided:	_____ correct	date: _____
Fourth try, student guided:	_____ correct	date: _____

Name: _____ Date: _____

Fluency Letter Page – "ar" and "ur

Point to the first letter and say the letter sound. Point to the second letter and say the letter sound. Repeat for each letter sound. Point to each word and say the word. Say "Your turn. You do what I did." Point to the first letter and say: "What does this say?" Point to the second letter and say: "What does this say?" Point to the third letter and say: "What does this say?" Repeat for each letter sound. Point to each word and say: "Read the word." Have reader repeat the whole process until words are easily read.

c	a	r	d		card
t	u	r	n		turn
b	u	r	n		burn
f	u	r	r	y	furry
h	u	r	r	y	hurry
h	a	r	d		hard

First try, teacher guided: _____ correct   date: _____

Second try, student guided: _____ correct   date: _____

Third try, student guided: _____ correct   date: _____

Fourth try, student guided: _____ correct   date: _____

44

Name: _____ Date: _____

Fluency – "ar" and "ur"

Read the passage aloud. Say: "Now it is your turn to read the passage."

Jed turned over the card.

It is Katie's turn to play.

The fire will burn the wood.

The dog was soft and furry.

I'm in a hurry to get home.

Turn the card over after I play.

The furry bunny hopped away.

He went after the furry bunny.

He caught the hurried bunny.

First try, teacher guided: _____ correct   date: _____
Second try, student guided: _____ correct   date: _____
Third try, student guided: _____ correct   date: _____
Fourth try, student guided: _____ correct   date: _____

Name: _____ Date: _____

Fluency Letter Page – "ow"

Point to the first letter and say the letter sound. Point to the second letter and say the letter sound. Repeat for each letter sound. Point to each word and say the word. Say "Your turn. You do what I did." Point to the first letter and say: "What does this say?" Point to the second letter and say: "What does this say?" Point to the third letter and say: "What does this say?" Repeat for each letter sound. Point to each word and say: "Read the word." Have reader repeat the whole process until words are easily read.

c	o	w	s		cows
s	n	o	w		snow
g	l	o	w		glow
g	r	o	w		grow
s	l	o	w		slow
b	r	o	w	n	brown

First try, teacher guided: _____ correct   date: _____

Second try, student guided: _____ correct   date: _____

Third try, student guided: _____ correct   date: _____

Fourth try, student guided: _____ correct   date: _____

Name: _____ Date: _____

Fluency – "ow"

Read the passage aloud. Say: "Now it is your turn to read the passage."

The cows drank the water.

The snow fell during winter.

The glow was bright and orange.

She will grow big and tall.

The slow truck was late.

Brown is the color of tree bark.

Slow down and move over.

The slow cow was brown.

The slow cow was in the snow.

First try, teacher guided:	_____ correct	date: _____
Second try, student guided:	_____ correct	date: _____
Third try, student guided:	_____ correct	date: _____
Fourth try, student guided:	_____ correct	date: _____

Passages

Name: _____ Date: _____

High Frequency Words

This is a one minute timed practice. When time is up calculate the total WPM read.

the	of	and	a	to	in	6
the	of	and	a	to	in	12
the	of	and	a	to	in	18
the	of	and	a	to	in	24
the	of	and	a	to	in	30
the	of	and	a	to	in	36
the	of	and	a	to	in	42
the	of	and	a	to	in	48
the	of	and	a	to	in	54
the	of	and	a	to	in	60
the	of	and	a	to	in	66
the	of	and	a	to	in	72
the	of	and	a	to	in	78
the	of	and	a	to	in	84
the	of	and	a	to	in	90
the	of	and	a	to	in	96
the	of	and	a	to	in	102
the	of	and	a	to	in	108

Total Words Read: _____
Minus errors: _____
= WPM _____

*Practice these words until you know them!

Name: _____ Date: _____

High Frequency Words 1

This is a **one minute** timed reading. When time is up calculate the total CWPM read by using the formula at the bottom of the page.

The boy put the ball in the box. The girl put the rope in	14
the box. The boy and the girl put the ball and the rope in	28
the box. The boy and the girl made the bed. The room was	41
now clean.	43
The boy put the ball in the box. The girl put the rope in	57
the box. The boy and the girl put the ball and the rope in	71
the box. The boy and the girl made the bed. The room was	84
now clean.	86
The boy put the ball in the box. The girl put the rope in	100
the box. The boy and the girl put the ball and the rope in	114
the box. The boy and the girl made the bed. The room was	127
now clean.	129
The boy put the ball in the box. The girl put the rope in	143
the box. The boy and the girl put the ball and the rope in	157
the box. The boy and the girl made the bed. The room was	170
now clean.	172

Total Words Read: _____
Minus errors: _____
= WPM   _____

Note: Mark the spot when time is up but let student finish reading the passage.

Name: _____ Date: _____

High Frequency Words 1 Comprehension

Please answer the questions using complete sentences.

1. Who put the ball in the box first? _____

_____

2. Where did the girl put the rope? _____

_____

3. What did the boy and the girl make? _____

_____

4. How many times does the passage repeat? _____

_____

5. Write two sentences telling what the passage is about. _____

_____

_____

Name: _____ Date: _____

High Frequency 2

This is a one minute timed practice. When time is up calculate the total WPM read.

is	you	that	it	he	was	6
is	you	that	it	he	was	12
is	you	that	it	he	was	18
is	you	that	it	he	was	24
is	you	that	it	he	was	30
is	you	that	it	he	was	36
is	you	that	it	he	was	42
is	you	that	it	he	was	48
is	you	that	it	he	was	54
is	you	that	it	he	was	60
is	you	that	it	he	was	66
is	you	that	it	he	was	72
is	you	that	it	he	was	78
is	you	that	it	he	was	84
is	you	that	it	he	was	90
is	you	that	it	he	was	96
is	you	that	it	he	was	102
is	you	that	it	he	was	108

Total Words Read: _____
Minus errors: _____
= WPM _____

*Practice these words until you know them!

Name: _____ Date: _____

High Frequency Words 2

This is a **one minute** timed reading. When time is up calculate the total CWPM read by using the formula at the bottom of the page.

It is time for him to go. He stayed too long. It was late	14
when he came. That is why he must go. It really is time for	28
him to go. He has work to do. He has stayed too long.	41
It is time for him to go. He stayed too long. It was late	55
when he came. That is why he must go. It really is time for	69
him to go. He has work to do. He has stayed too long.	82
It is time for him to go. He stayed too long. It was late	96
when he came. That is why he must go. It really is time for	110
him to go. He has work to do. He has stayed too long.	123
It is time for him to go. He stayed too long. It was late	137
when he came. That is why he must go. It really is time for	151
him to go. He has work to do. He has stayed too long.	164
It is time for him to go. He stayed too long. It was late	178
when he came. That is why he must go. It really is time for	192
him to go. He has work to do. He has stayed too long.	205

Total Words Read: _____
Minus errors: _____
= WPM _____

Note: Mark the spot when time is up but let student finish reading the passage.

Name: _____ Date: _____

High Frequency Words 2 Comprehension

Please answer the questions using complete sentences.

1. What is it time for him to do? _____

_____

2. Was it early or late when he came? _____

_____

3. Why is it time for him to go? _____

_____

4. Fill in the blanks:

_____ is time for him to go. He stayed too long. It was late

when _____ came. That is why he must _____. It really is

time for him to _____. He has work _____ do. He has stayed

too long.

5. Write two sentences telling what the passage is about. _____

_____

_____

Name: _____ Date: _____

Fluency "ir", "or" and "our"

This is a **one minute** timed reading. When time is up calculate the total CWPM read by using the formula at the bottom of the page.

For Sarah's birthday she wanted a giant cake shaped like	10
dirt. She also wanted gummy worms in it. Her family was	21
going to the shore for a party. Sarah thought a dirt cake	33
would be perfect for her outdoor party.	40
Before her birthday, her mother went to the store. She	50
asked the baker for a dirt cake. Sarah's mother did not	61
want to ignore Sarah's request.	66
The baker told her he could bake the cake. He told her	78
the worms would cost more money. Sarah's mother was fine	87
with that.	90
They picked up the cake. It was perfect. Brown chocolate	99
dirt and colorful worms. The cake even had green coconut	109
as weeds. It was perfect. It truly was a dirt cake.	121
They packed the cake and headed to the shore. They	131
arrived in a short time. They put on their skirts. They	142
greeted their guests and they ate dirt cake.	150

Total Words Read: _____
Minus errors: _____
= WPM _____

Note: Mark the spot when time is up but let student finish reading the passage.

Name: _____ Date: _____

Fluency "ir", "or" and "our"

Please answer the questions using complete sentences.

1. In what shape does Sarah want her cake? _____

_____

2. What kind of candy does Sarah want in her cake? _____

_____

3. Where is the party going to take place? _____

_____

4. What decision is Sarah's mother fine with? _____

_____

5. Describe Sarah's cake in detail. _____

_____

_____

_____

Name: _____ Date: _____

Fluency "long e spelled y"

This is a one minute timed practice. When time is up calculate the total WPM read.

baby	lady	very	only	many	penny	6
carry	sunny	bunny	puppy	dizzy	worry	12
baby	lady	very	only	many	penny	18
carry	sunny	bunny	puppy	dizzy	worry	24
baby	lady	very	only	many	penny	30
carry	sunny	bunny	puppy	dizzy	worry	36
baby	lady	very	only	many	penny	42
carry	sunny	bunny	puppy	dizzy	worry	48
baby	lady	very	only	many	penny	54
carry	sunny	bunny	puppy	dizzy	worry	60
baby	lady	very	only	many	penny	66
carry	sunny	bunny	puppy	dizzy	worry	72
baby	lady	very	only	many	penny	78
carry	sunny	bunny	puppy	dizzy	worry	84
baby	lady	very	only	many	penny	90
carry	sunny	bunny	puppy	dizzy	worry	96
baby	lady	very	only	many	penny	102
carry	sunny	bunny	puppy	dizzy	worry	108

Total Words Read: _____
Minus errors: _____
= WPM _____

*Practice these words until you know them!

Name: _____ Date: _____

Fluency "long e spelled y"

This is a **one minute** timed reading. When time is up calculate the total CWPM read by using the formula at the bottom of the page.

There was a very tall lady. She had a very tall baby. The	13
baby had a puppy. The baby and the puppy loved to play in	26
the sun. The puppy was happy when it was sunny. The	37
baby was happy when it was sunny.	44
One day they were playing outside and found a bunny. It	55
was a dizzy bunny. It was spinning in circles! It was funny	67
to see a bunny spin. The baby laughed. The puppy laughed.	78
It was very funny. The lady picked up the bunny.	88
"We will worry about this dizzy bunny if we do not take	100
him home," she said.	104
So they took the dizzy bunny home.	111
"I will carry him in my purse," the lady said.	121
The bunny sat in the purse. He sat on one penny and	133
two dimes. He looked out the top.	140
The baby and the puppy rode in the stroller. They were	151
happy walking home. It was a lucky day for them all.	162

Total Words Read: _____
Minus errors: _____
= WPM   _____

Note: Mark the spot when time is up but let student finish reading the passage.

Name: _____ Date: _____

Fluency "long e spelled y"

Please answer the questions using complete sentences.

1. How are the lady and the baby the same? _____
   _____

2. Which two characters loved to play in the sun? _____
   _____

3. What was the bunny doing that made them laugh? _____
   _____

4. Where did the lady carry the bunny? _____
   _____

5. Summarize the passage. _____
   _____
   _____
   _____

Name: _____ Date: _____

Fluency "contractions"

This is a one minute timed practice. When time is up calculate the total WPM read.

can't	don't	won't	wasn't	I'll	we'll	6
you'll	you'd	we'd	we've	hasn't	doesn't	12
can't	don't	won't	wasn't	I'll	we'll	18
you'll	you'd	we'd	we've	hasn't	doesn't	24
can't	don't	won't	wasn't	I'll	we'll	30
you'll	you'd	we'd	we've	hasn't	doesn't	36
can't	don't	won't	wasn't	I'll	we'll	42
you'll	you'd	we'd	we've	hasn't	doesn't	48
can't	don't	won't	wasn't	I'll	we'll	54
you'll	you'd	we'd	we've	hasn't	doesn't	60
can't	don't	won't	wasn't	I'll	we'll	66
you'll	you'd	we'd	we've	hasn't	doesn't	72
can't	don't	won't	wasn't	I'll	we'll	78
you'll	you'd	we'd	we've	hasn't	doesn't	84
can't	don't	won't	wasn't	I'll	we'll	90
you'll	you'd	we'd	we've	hasn't	doesn't	96
can't	don't	won't	wasn't	I'll	we'll	102
you'll	you'd	we'd	we've	hasn't	doesn't	108

Total Words Read: _____
Minus errors: _____
= WPM _____

*Practice these words until you know them!

Name: _____ Date: _____

Fluency "contractions"

This is a **one minute** timed reading. When time is up calculate the total CWPM read by using the formula at the bottom of the page.

I can't go to the game if I don't finish my work. I don't	14
want to finish my work. I want to go to the game.	26
I know! I'll pretend to finish my work. It doesn't matter if	38
I really do it. I won't get caught. I can't get caught.	50
All this was going through my head as I sat and tried to	63
figure out how to get to the game without doing my work.	75
Then I had an idea. I would ask my sister. We'd come up	88
with a plan. We've come up with plans before. We were	99
planners. Work hadn't stopped us from games before. Work	108
wouldn't stop us now. We'd come up with a plan and we	120
wouldn't have to work.	124
Then mom pointed out that I spent a lot of time planning	136
how not to work.	140
"You'd be finished with your work by now," she said, "if	151
you worked instead of planned on how to get out of work."	163
Mom had a point. Drat.	168

Total Words Read: _____
Minus errors: _____
= WPM _____

Note: Mark the spot when time is up but let student finish reading the passage.

Name: _____ Date: _____

Fluency "contractions"

Please answer the questions using complete sentences.

1. What must "I" do before going to the game? _____

_____

2. According to the passage, what can be done instead of finishing "my" work?

_____

3. Who will help come up with a plan? _____

_____

4. What point did mom make? _____

_____

5. Summarize the passage. _____

_____

_____

_____

Name: _____ Date: _____

Fluency "consonant pairs"

This is a one minute timed practice. When time is up calculate the total WPM read.

sweep	sheep	chime	brush	trip	chips	6
chill	broom	ship	crash	shove	swim	12
sweep	sheep	chime	brush	trip	chips	18
chill	broom	ship	crash	shove	swim	24
sweep	sheep	chime	brush	trip	chips	30
chill	broom	ship	crash	shove	swim	36
sweep	sheep	chime	brush	trip	chips	42
chill	broom	ship	crash	shove	swim	48
sweep	sheep	chime	brush	trip	chips	54
chill	broom	ship	crash	shove	swim	60
sweep	sheep	chime	brush	trip	chips	66
chill	broom	ship	crash	shove	swim	72
sweep	sheep	chime	brush	trip	chips	78
chill	broom	ship	crash	shove	swim	84
sweep	sheep	chime	brush	trip	chips	90
chill	broom	ship	crash	shove	swim	96
sweep	sheep	chime	brush	trip	chips	102
chill	broom	ship	crash	shove	swim	108

Total Words Read: _____
Minus errors: _____
= WPM   _____

*Practice these words until you know them!

Name: _____ Date: _____

Fluency "consonant pairs"

This is a **one minute** timed reading. When time is up calculate the total CWPM read by using the formula at the bottom of the page.

A ship full of sheep sailed the Pacific. They were on a	12
long trip to China.	16
Two days into the trip the ship crashed into another	26
ship. The crash was bad. It wrecked their boat. The sheep	37
had to swim to the other boat. They rushed through the	48
cold water. There was a chill in the air. The water was even	61
chillier.	62
On the other ship they were each given a broom. They	73
were told they had to sweep. They had to sweep for their	85
dinner of fish and chips. The sheep did not want to sweep.	97
Sheep don't eat fish and chips. They eat alfalfa and hay and	109
corn.	110
They were told to begin sweeping when the chime dinged.	120
They were told to stop when the second chimed dinged.	130
They swept for days, eating only fish and chips.	139
They were sure happy to get to China.	147

Total Words Read: _____
Minus errors: _____
= WPM _____

Note: Mark the spot when time is up but let student finish reading the passage.

Name: _____ Date: _____

Fluency "consonant pairs"

Please answer the questions using complete sentences.

1. What was the ship full of? _____

_____

2. Where did the ship sail? _____

_____

3. What did the sheep do when their ship crashed? _____

_____

4. According to the passage, what do sheep eat? _____

_____

5. Summarize the passage. _____

_____

_____

_____

Name: _____ Date: _____

Fluency "th"

This is a one minute timed practice. When time is up calculate the total WPM read.

they	them	this	that	these	those	6
both	other	cloth	thick	thin	with	12
they	them	this	that	these	those	18
both	other	cloth	thick	thin	with	24
they	them	this	that	these	those	30
both	other	cloth	thick	thin	with	36
they	them	this	that	these	those	42
both	other	cloth	thick	thin	with	48
they	them	this	that	these	those	54
both	other	cloth	thick	thin	with	60
they	them	this	that	these	those	66
both	other	cloth	thick	thin	with	72
they	them	this	that	these	those	78
both	other	cloth	thick	thin	with	84
they	them	this	that	these	those	90
both	other	cloth	thick	thin	with	96
they	them	this	that	these	those	102
both	other	cloth	thick	thin	with	108

Total Words Read: _____
Minus errors: _____
= WPM _____

*Practice these words until you know them!

Name: _____ Date: _____

Fluency "th"

This is a **one minute** timed reading. When time is up calculate the total CWPM read by using the formula at the bottom of the page.

Hannah likes shirts made with thick cloth in the winter.	10
They keep her warm and toasty. In the summer she likes	21
shirts made with thin cloth. They keep her cool and comfy.	32
She has two sets of clothes. Every Spring she puts away	43
her thick shirts. She wraps them up and puts them in the	55
garage. The time for those thick clothes is over as the	66
weather heats up.	69
Every Fall she puts away her thin clothes. She wraps	79
them up and covers them with tissue paper. These clothes	89
are done in late September when the days get chilly.	99
Her thick clothes are stylish. Her thin clothes are stylish.	108
Both sets are stylish; because, Hannah is a stylish person.	118

Total Words Read: _____
Minus errors: _____
= WPM _____

Note: Mark the spot when time is up but let student finish reading the passage.

Name: _____ Date: _____

Fluency "th"

Please answer the questions using complete sentences.

1. What shirts does Hannah like in the winter? _____
   _____

2. Describe Hannah's summer shirts? _____
   _____

3. When does Hannah put her summer shirts away? _____
   _____

4. What happens to the days in late September? _____
   _____

5. Summarize the passage in detail. _____
   _____
   _____
   _____

Name: _____ Date: _____

Fluency "-s" or "-es"

This is a one minute timed practice. When time is up calculate the total WPM read.

desk	desks	pencil	pencils	boy	boys	6
mess	messes	lunch	lunches	paint	paints	12
desk	desks	pencil	pencils	boy	boys	18
mess	messes	lunch	lunches	paint	paints	24
desk	desks	pencil	pencils	boy	boys	30
mess	messes	lunch	lunches	paint	paints	36
desk	desks	pencil	pencils	boy	boys	42
mess	messes	lunch	lunches	paint	paints	48
desk	desks	pencil	pencils	boy	boys	54
mess	messes	lunch	lunches	paint	paints	60
desk	desks	pencil	pencils	boy	boys	66
mess	messes	lunch	lunches	paint	paints	72
desk	desks	pencil	pencils	boy	boys	78
mess	messes	lunch	lunches	paint	paints	84
desk	desks	pencil	pencils	boy	boys	90
mess	messes	lunch	lunches	paint	paints	96
desk	desks	pencil	pencils	boy	boys	102
mess	messes	lunch	lunches	paint	paints	108

Total Words Read: _____
Minus errors: _____
= WPM _____

*Practice these words until you know them!

Name: _____ Date: _____

Fluency "-s" or "-es"

This is a **one minute** timed reading. When time is up calculate the total CWPM read by using the formula at the bottom of the page.

The boy sat in his desk. The girls sat in their desks too.	13
They were at their desks. The teacher explained what they	23
were doing next.	26
All of the children, the boy and the girls, were to take out	39
their pencils and some paper and put their name on the top.	50
Next, they were to explain the difference between the word	60
"mess" and "messes".	63
A girl named Joel decided she would show the difference.	73
She got out her paints. She used the blue paint and the red	86
paint to scribble on the paper. Under it she wrote mess.	97
She spilled yellow paint on her desk. She wrote "messes"	107
next to the paper and her desk. There were two messes, she	119
thought, one on the paper and one on the desk.	129
While the other children got to eat their lunches outside,	139
Joel got to eat her lunch in the office with the principal.	151
After she cleaned up both messes.	157

Total Words Read: _____
Minus errors: _____
= WPM _____

Note: Mark the spot when time is up but let student finish reading the passage.

Name: _____ Date: _____

Fluency "-s or -es"

Please answer the questions using complete sentences.

1. Where did the children sit? _____
_____

2. What did the teacher explain? _____
_____

3. Who decided she would show the difference? _____
_____

4. What did she do? _____
_____

5. Summarize the passage. _____
_____
_____
_____

Name: _____ Date: _____

Fluency soft "c" and "s"

This is a one minute timed practice. When time is up calculate the total WPM read.

six	ask	ice	price	slice	city	6
face	fence	since	soft	place	piece	12
six	ask	ice	price	slice	city	18
face	fence	since	soft	place	piece	24
six	ask	ice	price	slice	city	30
face	fence	since	soft	place	piece	36
six	ask	ice	price	slice	city	42
face	fence	since	soft	place	piece	48
six	ask	ice	price	slice	city	54
face	fence	since	soft	place	piece	60
six	ask	ice	price	slice	city	66
face	fence	since	soft	place	piece	72
six	ask	ice	price	slice	city	78
face	fence	since	soft	place	piece	84
six	ask	ice	price	slice	city	90
face	fence	since	soft	place	piece	96
six	ask	ice	price	slice	city	102
face	fence	since	soft	place	piece	108

Total Words Read: _____
Minus errors: _____
= WPM _____

*Practice these words until you know them!

Name: _____   Date: _____

Fluency soft "c" and "s"

This is a **one minute** timed reading. When time is up calculate the total CWPM read by using the formula at the bottom of the page.

Six ice cubes sat on the fence outside the city. The piece	12
of fence they sat on was sitting in the summer sun. The ice	25
cubes cost three cents each. The price was high, but they	36
were used to keep the slice of pie cool and Sal could not live	50
without his slice of pie.	55
The store, on the edge of the city, was a mile from the	68
fence. The store sold the best berry pie. If you wanted berry	80
pie, that was the place to get it. The pie melted in your	93
mouth. The crust was crisp and the filling soft and yummy.	104
Sal liked his pie ice cold. Since Sal had to walk home	116
with the pie, he needed the ice. Every afternoon, Sal went to	128
the store. He asked for a piece of pie. He walked home. He	141
sat on his fence. He put the ice aside and he ate the pie.	155
It was a slice of berry heaven.	162

Total Words Read: _____
Minus errors: _____
= WPM   _____

Note: Mark the spot when time is up but let student finish reading the passage.

Name: _____ Date: _____

Fluency "soft c and s"

Please answer the questions using complete sentences.

1. What was on the fence? _____

   _____

2. How much did each ice cube cost? _____

   _____

3. What kind of pie did the store sell? _____

   _____

4. According to the passage, who ate the pie? _____

   _____

5. Summarize the passage. _____

   _____

   _____

   _____

Name: _____ Date: _____

Fluency "compound words"

This is a one minute timed practice. When time is up calculate the total WPM read.

bedroom	into	bulldog	cupcake	without	sometime	6
maybe	myself	football	softball	bathroom	anything	12
bedroom	into	bulldog	cupcake	without	sometime	18
maybe	myself	football	softball	bathroom	anything	24
bedroom	into	bulldog	cupcake	without	sometime	30
maybe	myself	football	softball	bathroom	anything	36
bedroom	into	bulldog	cupcake	without	sometime	42
maybe	myself	football	softball	bathroom	anything	48
bedroom	into	bulldog	cupcake	without	sometime	54
maybe	myself	football	softball	bathroom	anything	60
bedroom	into	bulldog	cupcake	without	sometime	66
maybe	myself	football	softball	bathroom	anything	72
bedroom	into	bulldog	cupcake	without	sometime	78
maybe	myself	football	softball	bathroom	anything	84
bedroom	into	bulldog	cupcake	without	sometime	90
maybe	myself	football	softball	bathroom	anything	96
bedroom	into	bulldog	cupcake	without	sometime	102
maybe	myself	football	softball	bathroom	anything	108

Total Words Read: _____
Minus errors: _____
= WPM _____

*Practice these words until you know them!

Name: _____ Date: _____

Fluency "compound words"

This is a **one minute** timed reading. When time is up calculate the total CWPM read by using the formula at the bottom of the page.

I walked out of the bedroom. It was dark. I could not see	13
anything. I was headed to the kitchen for a cupcake. They	24
were chocolate. I love chocolate cupcakes.	30
The cupcakes were for the Bullfrog bake sale. My school	40
mascot is a bullfrog. We were raising money for our football	51
and softball teams.	54
The teams are broke. They need money badly. Without	63
money to hire referees and coaches no one gets to play. That	75
would be sad.	78
I baked the cupcakes myself. I don't think one will be	89
missed. I made a quick stop at the bathroom before heading	100
into the kitchen.	103
I turned on the stove light. It was soft. It cast a glow	116
above my cupcakes. I took a deep breath. They were	126
perfect. Sometimes I amaze myself. I ate my cupcake and	136
went back to bed.	140

Total Words Read: _____
Minus errors: _____
= WPM _____

Note: Mark the spot when time is up but let student finish reading the passage.

Name: _____ Date: _____

Fluency "compound words"

Please answer the questions using complete sentences.

1. What was the person in the passage doing? _____

   _____

2. Describe the cupcakes? _____

   _____

3. What were the cupcakes for? _____

   _____

4. Where did the narrator stop before heading into the kitchen? _____

   _____

5. Summarize the passage. _____

   _____

   _____

   _____

Name: _____ Date: _____

Fluency "f", "ff" and "ough"

This is a 60 second timed practice. When time is up calculate the total WPM read.

flip	flop	flew	muffin	five	four	6
family	cough	far	cliff	stuff	off	12
flip	flop	flew	muffin	five	four	18
family	cough	far	cliff	stuff	off	24
flip	flop	flew	muffin	five	four	30
family	cough	far	cliff	stuff	off	36
flip	flop	flew	muffin	five	four	42
family	cough	far	cliff	stuff	off	48
flip	flop	flew	muffin	five	four	54
family	cough	far	cliff	stuff	off	60
flip	flop	flew	muffin	five	four	66
family	cough	far	cliff	stuff	off	72
flip	flop	flew	muffin	five	four	78
family	cough	far	cliff	stuff	off	84
flip	flop	flew	muffin	five	four	90
family	cough	far	cliff	stuff	off	96
flip	flop	flew	muffin	five	four	102
family	cough	far	cliff	stuff	off	108

Total Words Read: _____
Minus errors: _____
= WPM   _____

*Practice these words until you know them!

Name: _____ Date: _____

Fluency "f", "ff" and "ough"

This is a **one minute** timed reading. When time is up calculate the total CWPM read by using the formula at the bottom of the page.

Jake and his family lived on a cliff. The cliff overlooked	11
the ocean. When Jake was four he started jumping off the	22
cliff into the ocean. He did it four or five times a day.	35
Sometimes he did back flips. Sometimes he did front	44
flips. Sometimes he did belly flops right into the water.	54
The cliff was high. The water was far below. Jake knew	65
the water was deep, so he was safe. He liked the feeling of	78
flying over the edge. It was the stuff of dreams. The feeling	90
of flying like a falcon. He loved it.	98
His mother would watch him jump off the cliff. She	108
watched him flip and she watched him flop. She waited at	119
the top of the cliff with fresh muffins. Jake loved his mom's	131
muffins. They were the perfect fuel for his flipping and	141
flopping.	142
On his last flight of the day, Jake would jump. He flew	154
through the air and raced to the top of the cliff for mom's	167
muffins. The perfect end to a perfect day.	175

Total Words Read: _____
Minus errors: _____
= WPM   _____

Note: Mark the spot when time is up but let student finish reading the passage.

Name: _____ Date: _____

Fluency "f, ff and ough"

Please answer the questions using complete sentences.

1. Where did Jake and his family live? _____

   _____

2. What did Jake do off of the cliff? _____

   _____

3. What was the stuff of dreams? _____

   _____

4. What did Jake's mother do? Please use details. _____

   _____

5. Summarize the passage. _____

   _____

   _____

   _____

Name: _____ Date: _____

Fluency "w", "wh" and "h"

This is a one minute timed practice. When time is up calculate the total WPM read.

hold	hips	has	help	water	wish	6
willing	when	while	who	what	where	12
hold	hips	has	help	water	wish	18
willing	when	while	who	what	where	24
hold	hips	has	help	water	wish	30
willing	when	while	who	what	where	36
hold	hips	has	help	water	wish	42
willing	when	while	who	what	where	48
hold	hips	has	help	water	wish	54
willing	when	while	who	what	where	60
hold	hips	has	help	water	wish	66
willing	when	while	who	what	where	72
hold	hips	has	help	water	wish	78
willing	when	while	who	what	where	84
hold	hips	has	help	water	wish	90
willing	when	while	who	what	where	96
hold	hips	has	help	water	wish	102
willing	when	while	who	what	where	108

Total Words Read: _____
Minus errors: _____
= WPM _____

*Practice these words until you know them!

Name: _____ Date: _____

Fluency "w", "wh" and "h"

This is a **one minute** timed reading. When time is up calculate the total CWPM read by using the formula at the bottom of the page.

Han put her hands on her hips and said, "I will not go	13
into the house!"	16
Han didn't care who wanted her to go inside. She didn't	27
care what they said. She wanted to stay outside and play in	39
the water.	41
Han's mom called her again. "Dinner is ready. Come	51
and eat."	52
Han was not willing to go inside. Her mother appeared	63
at the door. "Young lady," she said, "you come in this house	74
and get ready for dinner."	79
Han held her breath. She did not wish to go inside.	90
"Okay, then no dessert for you."	96
No dessert, Han thought. "What is for dessert?" she	105
asked.	106
"Chocolate cupcakes."	108
Han zoomed inside.	111

Total Words Read: _____
Minus errors: _____
= WPM _____

Note: Mark the spot when time is up but let student finish reading the passage.

Name: _____ Date: _____

Fluency "w, wh, and h"

Please answer the questions using complete sentences.

1. What did Han say with her hands on her hips? _____

_____

2. Why did Han want to stay outside? _____

_____

3. Why was her mother calling Han? _____

_____

4. What made Han decide to go inside? _____

_____

5. Summarize the passage. _____

_____

_____

_____

Name: _____ Date: _____

Fluency "More High Frequency Words"

This is a one minute timed practice. When time is up calculate the total WPM read.

the	of	and	a	to	in	6
is	you	that	it	he	for	12
was	on	are	as	with	his	18
they	at	be	this	from	I	24
have	or	by	one	had	not	30
but	what	all	were	when	we	36
there	can	an	your	which	if	42
said	do	will	each	about	how	48
up	out	them	then	she	many	54
the	of	and	a	to	in	60
is	you	that	it	he	for	66
was	on	are	as	with	his	72
they	at	be	this	from	I	78
have	or	by	one	had	not	84
but	what	all	were	when	we	90
there	can	an	your	which	if	96
said	do	will	each	about	how	102
up	out	them	then	she	many	108

Total Words Read: _____
Minus errors: _____
= WPM _____

*Practice these words until you know them!

Name: _____ Date: _____

Fluency "More High Frequency Words"

This is a **one minute** timed reading. When time is up calculate the total CWPM read by using the formula at the bottom of the page.

The boy and his dog went to the park. They were playing	12
in the sand. It was a warm day and the sand was hot.	25
They met a girl named Sarah. She was nice. They asked	36
her if she would like to play with them. They all played	48
together on the hot sand. Each of them had a small shovel.	60
"Can you dig a deep hole?" the boy asked.	69
"I can dig many deep holes," she said.	77
They were digging holes, which were quite deep. The	86
sand was by a pond. They decided to fill the holes with	98
water. The dog would not let them. He kept splashing in the	110
holes.	111
From out of nowhere came an enormous bee. The bee	121
stung the dog on his nose many times. The dog was sad.	133
The boy took him home. He put ice on the dog's nose.	145
The dog felt better.	149
They went back to the park the very next day.	159

Total Words Read: _____
Minus errors: _____
= WPM   _____

Note: Mark the spot when time is up but let student finish reading the passage.

Name: _____ Date: _____

Fluency "More High Frequency Words"

Please answer the questions using complete sentences.

1. Where did the boy and his do go? _____

   _____

2. Who did the boy and his dog meet at the park? _____

   _____

3. What did they do at the park? _____

   _____

4. What came out of no where? _____

   _____

5. Summarize the passage. _____

   _____

   _____

   _____

Name: _____ Date: _____

Fluency "Even More High Frequency Words"

This is a sixty second timed practice. When time is up calculate the total WPM read.

some	so	these	would	other	into	6
has	more	her	two	like	him	12
see	time	could	no	make	than	18
first	been	its	who	now	people	24
my	made	over	did	down	only	30
some	so	these	would	other	into	36
has	more	her	two	like	him	42
see	time	could	no	make	than	48
first	been	its	who	now	people	54
my	made	over	did	down	only	60
some	so	these	would	other	into	66
has	more	her	two	like	him	72
see	time	could	no	make	than	78
first	been	its	who	now	people	84
my	made	over	did	down	only	90
some	so	these	would	other	into	96
has	more	her	two	like	him	102
see	time	could	no	make	than	108
first	been	its	who	now	people	114
my	made	over	did	down	only	120

Total Words Read: _____
Minus errors: _____
= WPM _____

*Practice these words until you know them!

Name: _____ Date: _____

Fluency "Even High Frequency Words"

This is a **one minute** timed reading. When time is up calculate the total CWPM read by using the formula at the bottom of the page.

Some people like to read. Jessi was one of those people.	11
To her, there was nothing better than a good book. The only	23
problem was – once she picked one up she did not want to	35
put it down. No one could make her either.	44
She would spend hours reading, first with one book and	54
then with another. Her favorite books were about princes	63
and princesses. She was really into them.	70
Jessi read when she sat. She read when she walked.	80
Jessi even read when she ate dinner.	87
No one could get Jessi to do anything but read. She did	99
it all of the time. Until one day when she was reading and	112
fell off a curb. Now, Jessi only reads when she is sitting	124
down.	125

Total Words Read: _____
Minus errors: _____
= WPM   _____

Note: Mark the spot when time is up, but let student finish reading the passage.

Name: _____ Date: _____

Fluency "Even More High Frequency Words"

Please answer the questions using complete sentences.

1. According to the passage, what does Jessi like to do? _____
_____

2. According to the passage, what is the problem with good books? _____
_____

3. What were Jessi's favorite books about? _____
_____

4. What made Jessi decide to only read sitting down? _____
_____

5. Summarize the passage. _____
_____
_____
_____

Name: _____ Date: _____

Fluency "Words, Words, Words"

This is a one minute timed practice. When time is up calculate the total WPM read.

can	dog	and	lot	swim	lake	6
gets	dock	summer	jump	dash	race	12
spent	the	in	run	hop	met	18
jump	jumping	jumped	dash	dashing	dashed	24
race	racing	raced	place	placing	placed	30
play	playing	played	stay	staying	stayed	36
can	dog	and	lot	swim	lake	42
gets	dock	summer	jump	dash	race	48
spent	the	in	run	hop	met	54
jump	jumping	jumped	dash	dashing	dashed	60
race	racing	raced	place	placing	placed	66
play	playing	played	stay	staying	stayed	72
can	dog	and	lot	swim	lake	78
gets	dock	summer	jump	dash	race	84
spent	the	in	run	hop	met	90
jump	jumping	jumped	dash	dashing	dashed	96
race	racing	raced	place	placing	placed	102
play	playing	played	stay	staying	stayed	108
can	dog	and	lot	swim	lake	114
gets	dock	summer	jump	dash	race	120

Total Words Read: _____
Minus errors: _____
= WPM _____

*Practice these words until you know them!

Name: _____ Date: _____

Fluency "Words, Words, Words"

This is a **one minute** timed reading. When time is up calculate the total CWPM read by using the formula at the bottom of the page.

Jeff met his friend Jake at the lake. They loved going to the lake on hot	16
summer days. Jake always brought his dog. The three played and played.	28
The three, Jeff, Jake and Jake's dog Topper, spent the days jumping	40
off of the dock. They jumped out far. They raced back to the dock and	55
jumped again. Over and over they played.	62
One day, while they were playing, another dog hopped onto the dock	74
with them. He was a friendly dog. The name on the dog's tag was Meg.	89
Meg stayed with the boys and Topper all day long. She sat on the dock	104
while they played. She sat on the dock while they jumped. She even sat	118
on the dock when Topper rushed in and out of the water.	130
At three o'clock, the boys put on their clothes. It was time to go home.	145
They jumped from the dock to the dirt. Meg followed them. They crossed	158
the lot to their houses. Meg followed them.	165
"Where do you live girl?" Jeff asked Meg.	173
She lifted her ears and gave him a lick.	182
"What do you think we should do?" Jake asked Jeff.	192
"I would like to take her home," Jake said. Meg wagged her tail.	204
The boys took Meg to Jake's house. Jake's mom would not let him	217
keep her. They made flyers. They put them up. The next day Meg's owner	231
came to get her. Meg's owner was a girl from Jeff and Jake's class named	146
Kate.	147
Jeff and Jake invited Kate and Meg to go swimming with them. The	160
did.	161

Total Words Read: _____
Minus errors: _____
= WPM   _____

Note: Mark the spot when time is up, but let student finish reading the passage.

Name: _____ Date: _____

Fluency "Words, Words, Words"

Please answer the questions using complete sentences.

1. Who did Jeff meet by the lake? _____

_____

2. How did Jeff and Topper spend their days? _____

_____

3. What did they do at three o'clock? _____

_____

4. How did they find Meg's owners? _____

_____

5. Summarize the passage. _____

_____

_____

_____

Name: _____   Date: _____

Fluency "Words Again!"

This is a one minute timed practice. When time is up calculate the total WPM read.

yet	beg	can	net	pet	fast	6
run	jump	swim	fly	dog	cat	12
bird	fish	duck	bugs	catch	wait	18
yet	beg	can	net	pet	fast	24
run	jump	swim	fly	dog	cat	30
bird	fish	duck	bugs	catch	wait	36
yet	beg	can	net	pet	fast	42
run	jump	swim	fly	dog	cat	48
bird	fish	duck	bugs	catch	wait	54
yet	beg	can	net	pet	fast	60
run	jump	swim	fly	dog	cat	66
bird	fish	duck	bugs	catch	wait	72
yet	beg	can	net	pet	fast	78
run	jump	swim	fly	dog	cat	84
bird	fish	duck	bugs	catch	wait	90
yet	beg	can	net	pet	fast	96
run	jump	swim	fly	dog	cat	102
bird	fish	duck	bugs	catch	wait	108
yet	beg	can	net	pet	fast	114
run	jump	swim	fly	dog	cat	120

Total Words Read: _____
Minus errors: _____
= WPM _____

*Practice these words until you know them!

Name: _____ Date: _____

Fluency "Words Again"

This is a **one minute** timed reading. When time is up calculate the total CWPM read by using the formula at the bottom of the page.

Many people have pets. People have dogs for pets. People have cats for	13
pets. People have birds for pets. People even have fish for pets.	25
Pets can do different things. Some pets can jump. Some pets can beg.	38
Some pets can swim. Some pets can fly.	46
Some pets can jump and beg. Some pets can beg and swim. Some	59
pets can fly and swim. Do you know of any pets who can jump, beg and	75
fly?	76
A dog can jump and beg. A dog can beg and swim. A duck can fly and	93
swim. Can a cat fly and swim? Cats don't usually like water? Cats may	107
not be able to fly and swim, but they sure can jump!	119
Some fish can jump. Fish jump out of the water to catch bugs. Fish	133
jump out of the water to play. Fish in tanks can jump out of the water if	150
the water is bad! That is not a good thing.	160
Some people have pets that are very fast. Dogs can be very fast. Cats	174
can be very fast. Fish can be very fast. Even ducks can be very fast.	189
Most pets can run. Dogs can run. Cats can run. Ducks can run. Wait,	203
how did ducks get in our pet list? Can fish run? Only in cartoons or	218
books!	219
Many people have pets. Do you?	225

Total Words Read: _____
Minus errors: _____
= WPM _____

Note: Mark the spot when time is up, but let student finish reading the passage.

Name: _____ Date: _____

Fluency "Words Again"

Please answer the questions using complete sentences.

1. According to the passage, what kind of pets do people have? _____
   _____

2. List some of the things the passage says dogs do? _____
   _____

3. According to the passage, what can some fish do? _____
   _____

4. What can run but is not on the pet list? _____
   _____

5. Summarize the passage. _____
   _____
   _____
   _____

Name: _____ Date: _____

Fluency "Words Revisited"

This is a one minute timed practice. When time is up calculate the total WPM read.

rat	big	can	run	jump	fast	6
tail	world	buck	smarter	white	gray	12
black	some	the	know	body	friends	18
they	lonely	have	never	forget	will	24
rat	big	can	run	jump	fast	30
tail	world	buck	smarter	white	gray	36
black	some	the	know	body	friends	42
they	lonely	have	never	forget	will	48
rat	big	can	run	jump	fast	54
tail	world	buck	smarter	white	gray	60
black	some	the	know	body	friends	66
they	lonely	have	never	forget	will	72
rat	big	can	run	jump	fast	78
tail	world	buck	smarter	white	gray	84
black	some	the	know	body	friends	90
they	lonely	have	never	forget	will	96
rat	big	can	run	jump	fast	102
tail	world	buck	smarter	white	gray	108
black	some	the	know	body	friends	114
they	lonely	have	never	forget	will	120

Total Words Read: _____
Minus errors: _____
= WPM _____

*Practice these words until you know them!

Name: _____ Date: _____

Fluency "Words Revisited"

This is a **one minute** timed reading. When time is up calculate the total CWPM read by using the formula at the bottom of the page.

Rats are mammals. Rats can be found all over the world. Some rats	13
are small. Some rats are big. Rats can be white. Rats can be black. Rats	28
can be gray.	31
Rats have sharp claws. Rats have ears that stick straight up. They	44
have long tails. Did you know rats use their tails to control their body	58
temperature?	59
Male rats are known as bucks. Female rats are known as does. Does	72
is pronounced like toes.	76
Rats have leaders. The leaders are the largest rats. The leaders are	88
also the strongest rats. The largest and strongest rats get the best food.	101
The largest and strongest rats get the best places to live.	112
Rats are lovable. They like being in groups with other rats. Pet rats	125
like being with their humans. Did you know that when rats don't have	138
friends they get lonely?	142
Rats are smart. Rats are smarter than mice. Rats are smarter than	154
rabbits. Rats have great memories. Once a rat learns how to get	166
someplace he will never forget.	171
Have you ever seen a rat?	177

Total Words Read: _____
Minus errors: _____
= WPM   _____

Note: Mark the spot when time is up, but let student finish reading the passage.

Name: _____ Date: _____

Fluency "Words Revisited"

Please answer the questions using complete sentences.

1. According to the passage, what are rats? _____
_____

2. Describe a rat? _____
_____

3. According to the passage, what are female rats called? _____
_____

4. Describe a rat leader? _____
_____

5. Summarize the passage. _____
_____
_____
_____

Name: _____ Date: _____

Fluency "More Words to Read"

This is a one minute timed practice. When time is up calculate the total WPM read.

jet	fly	high	low	sits	pilot	6
grab	blasts	past	never	fast	things	12
hours	pilot	through	been	first	yell	18
ready	want	met	first	house	look	24
jet	fly	high	low	sits	pilot	30
grab	blasts	past	never	fast	things	36
hours	pilot	through	been	first	yell	42
ready	want	met	first	house	look	48
jet	fly	high	low	sits	pilot	54
grab	blasts	past	never	fast	things	60
hours	pilot	through	been	first	yell	66
ready	want	met	first	house	look	72
jet	fly	high	low	sits	pilot	78
grab	blasts	past	never	fast	things	84
hours	pilot	through	been	first	yell	90
ready	want	met	first	house	look	96
jet	fly	high	low	sits	pilot	102
grab	blasts	past	never	fast	things	108
hours	pilot	through	been	first	yell	114
ready	want	met	first	house	look	120

Total Words Read: _____
Minus errors: _____
= WPM _____

*Practice these words until you know them!

Name: _____ Date: _____

Fluency "More Words to Read"

This is a **one minute** timed reading. When time is up calculate the total CWPM read by using the formula at the bottom of the page.

Jade likes to fly jets. Jade likes to fly jets high. Jade likes to fly jets	16
low. Jade likes to fly jets high and low. Jade sits in her pilot chair. She	32
grabs the throttle and gets ready to fly.	40
Just before she takes off, Jade yells, "ready, set, go." Then swoosh!	52
She is off and flying.	57
Up in the sky, Jade blasts past the birds. Up in the sky, Jade flies fast	73
and first. Last place is not the place for a jet pilot. I have never met a pilot	91
of jets who did not want to fly fast. I have never met a pilot of jets who did	110
not want to land first.	115
Jade sees all sorts of things when she flies. She sees rivers that look	129
like strings. She sees trees that look like dots. She sees houses that look	143
very small. Jade sees rivers, trees and houses from way up high.	155
It took a long time for Jade to become a pilot. She had to practice	170
flying. She had to fly with an instructor. She had to fly solo. She had to	186
fly and fly for many hours before she became a pilot.	197
Jade loves to fly her jets. Jade loves to sail through the big blue sky.	212
Have you ever been on a jet?	219

Total Words Read: _____
Minus errors: _____
= WPM _____

Note: Mark the spot when time is up, but let student finish reading the passage.

Name: _____ Date: _____

Fluency "More Words to Read"

Please answer the questions using complete sentences.

1. According to the passage, what does Jade like to fly? _____

_____

2. What does Jade yell before he takes off? _____

_____

3. What does Jade see when she flies? _____

_____

4. According to Jade, what do all pilots want to do? _____

_____

5. Summarize the passage. _____

_____

_____

_____

Name: _____ Date: _____

Fluency – The Other Sound of C

This is a one minute timed practice. When time is up calculate the total WPM read.

cent	city	cycle	space	civil	cellar	6
pencil	fancy	celery	center	price	fence	12
dance	slice	face	lace	mice	twice	18
cent	city	cycle	space	civil	cellar	24
pencil	fancy	celery	center	price	fence	30
dance	slice	face	lace	mice	twice	36
cent	city	cycle	space	civil	cellar	42
pencil	fancy	celery	center	price	fence	48
dance	slice	face	lace	mice	twice	54
cent	city	cycle	space	civil	cellar	60
pencil	fancy	celery	center	price	fence	66
dance	slice	face	lace	mice	twice	72
cent	city	cycle	space	civil	cellar	78
pencil	fancy	celery	center	price	fence	84
dance	slice	face	lace	mice	twice	90
cent	city	cycle	space	civil	cellar	96
pencil	fancy	celery	center	price	fence	102
dance	slice	face	lace	mice	twice	108
cent	city	cycle	space	civil	cellar	114
pencil	fancy	celery	center	price	fence	120

Total Words Read: _____
Minus errors: _____
= WPM _____

*Practice these words until you know them!

Name: _____ Date: _____

Fluency – The Other Sound of C

This is a **one minute** timed reading. When time is up calculate the total CWPM read by using the formula at the bottom of the page.

The letter "C" makes two sounds. The letter "C" can sound hard like in	14
"cat". The letter "C" can sound soft like in "cent".	24
It is important to know the rules for when the letter "C" sounds hard.	37
It is important to know the rules for when the letter "C" sounds soft.	51
The letter "C" sounds soft when it is followed by e, I, or y. In the word	68
cent, the letter "C" is followed by an e. Is the "C" hard or soft? It is soft	86
because it is followed by an e. In the word city, is the letter "C" hard or	103
soft. It is soft because it is followed by a y.	114
There are many soft "C" words. Space is a soft "C" word. Cellar is a	129
soft "C" word. Pencil, fancy and celery are all soft "C" words.	141
There are other words that have the soft "C" sound. Celery and center	154
both have the soft "C" sound. Dance, lace, slice, face, place and cyclone	167
all have the soft "C" sound.	173
When you read cat and price, can you tell which is the soft "C" sound?	188
How about when you read fence and creep? Can you tell which one is the	203
soft "C"? How many soft "C" words can you name? Ready. Go!	215

Total Words Read: _____
Minus errors: _____
= WPM _____

Note: Mark the spot when time is up, but let student finish reading the passage.

Name: _____ Date: _____

Fluency "The Other Sound of C"

Please answer the questions using complete sentences.

1. What sounds does the letter C make? _____
_____

2. What is the soft C rule? _____
_____

3. Is the C in the word "city" hard or soft? _____
_____

4. Name three words in the passage with hard C sounds? _____
_____

5. Summarize the passage. _____
_____
_____
_____

Name: _____   Date: _____

Fluency "Almost Last Set of Words"

This is a one minute timed practice. When time is up calculate the total WPM read.

earth	rocks	home	water	trees	houses	6
rivers	lakes	paper	furniture	wood	drink	12
people	think	yards	big	pathways	ourselves	18
electricity	furniture	make	kitchen	build	dishes	24
earth	rocks	home	water	trees	houses	30
rivers	lakes	paper	furniture	wood	drink	36
people	think	yards	big	pathways	ourselves	42
electricity	furniture	make	kitchen	build	dishes	48
earth	rocks	home	water	trees	houses	54
rivers	lakes	paper	furniture	wood	drink	60
people	think	yards	big	pathways	ourselves	66
electricity	furniture	make	kitchen	build	dishes	72
earth	rocks	home	water	trees	houses	78
rivers	lakes	paper	furniture	wood	drink	84
people	think	yards	big	pathways	ourselves	90
electricity	furniture	make	kitchen	build	dishes	96
earth	rocks	home	water	trees	houses	102
rivers	lakes	paper	furniture	wood	drink	108
people	think	yards	big	pathways	ourselves	114
electricity	furniture	make	kitchen	build	dishes	120

Total Words Read: _____
Minus errors: _____
= WPM _____

*Practice these words until you know them!

Name: _____ Date: _____

Fluency "Almost Last Set of Words" Passage

This is a **one minute** timed reading. When time is up calculate the total CWPM read by using the formula at the bottom of the page.

Our earth is where we live. Our earth is our home. The earth is also	15
home to trees. The earth is home to rocks. The earth is home to rivers	30
and lakes as well. Trees, rocks, rivers and lakes are all used by people.	44
People use trees for their wood. To get wood we cut down trees. We	58
use the wood to make houses. We use the wood to make furniture. We	72
even use the wood to make paper. Can you think of other things that are	87
made out of wood?	91
Rocks are used by people for many things. Some rocks are big. Big	104
rocks are often cut and used in our homes. We make kitchen countertops	117
out of huge rocks that are cut. We use rocks to make fireplaces and	131
pathways through our yards. We even use rocks to build with. Can you	144
think of other things we use rocks to make?	153
Rivers and lakes are full of water. Water is one of the most important	167
things we use. We use water to drink. We use water to clean our dishes	182
and ourselves. We even use water to make electricity. Can you think of	195
other ways we use water?	200

Total Words Read: _____
Minus errors: _____
= WPM _____

Note: Mark the spot when time is up, but let student finish reading the passage.

Name: _____ Date: _____

Fluency "Almost Last Set of Words"

Please answer the questions using complete sentences.

1. According to the passage, what is the earth home to? _____
_____

2. According to the passage, what do people use trees for? _____
_____

3. According to the passage, what are rocks used for? _____
_____

4. According to the passage, what are sources of water? _____
_____

5. Summarize the passage. _____
_____
_____
_____

Name: _____ Date: _____

Fluency "Last Set of Words"

This is a one minute timed practice. When time is up calculate the total WPM read.

hero	think	police	officer	brave	very	6
people	animal	care	special	give	sights	12
sounds	busy	make	better	learn	dog	18
hear	disability	smell	train	trained	highly	24
hero	think	police	officer	brave	very	30
people	animal	care	special	give	sights	36
sounds	busy	make	better	learn	dog	42
hear	disability	smell	train	trained	highly	48
hero	think	police	officer	brave	very	54
people	animal	care	special	give	sights	60
sounds	busy	make	better	learn	dog	66
hear	disability	smell	train	trained	highly	72
hero	think	police	officer	brave	very	78
people	animal	care	special	give	sights	84
sounds	busy	make	better	learn	dog	90
hear	disability	smell	train	trained	highly	96
hero	think	police	officer	brave	very	102
people	animal	care	special	give	sights	108
sounds	busy	make	better	learn	dog	114
hear	disability	smell	train	trained	highly	120

Total Words Read: _____
Minus errors: _____
= WPM _____

*Practice these words until you know them!

Name: _____   Date: _____

Fluency "Last Set of Words "Passage

This is a **one minute** timed reading. When time is up calculate the total CWPM read by using the formula at the bottom of the page.

When we think of heroes we think of firefighters. When we think of	13
heroes we think of police officers. Both police officers and firefighters	24
help others. Both police officers are firefighters are very brave. But if you	37
think about it – dogs can be heroes too.	45
Animals help people. They keep us company. They are our friends.	56
Some animals help people with disabilities. Some help save lives and	67
some give special care to people!	73
Hearing ear dogs, help people who are deaf or who can't hear well.	86
These dogs are trained to listen for sounds. They alert their owners to	99
important sounds. They help keep their owners safe.	107
Guide dogs help people who are blind or who can't see very well. A	121
guide dog learns the sights of busy places. Guide dogs learn the sounds	134
of busy places. Guide dogs learn the smells of busy places. They are	147
highly trained. They are trained to follow directions from their owners.	158
Some guide dogs save lives. There are stories of guide dogs helping	170
their people out of burning buildings. Animals can not only make our	182
lives better, but they are our heroes as well!	191

Total Words Read: _____
Minus errors: _____
= WPM _____

Note: Mark the spot when time is up, but let student finish reading the passage.

Name: _____ Date: _____

Fluency "Last Set of Words"

Please answer the questions using complete sentences.

1. According to the passage, what do we think of when we hear heroes? _____

_____

2. According to the passage, what, besides people, can be heroes? _____

_____

3. How do dogs help people? _____

_____

4. Describe some of the ways the passage claims dogs help people? _____

_____

5. Summarize the passage. _____

_____

_____

_____

Name: _____ Date: _____

Fluency Practice – Action Words

This is a 60 second timed practice. When time is up calculate the total WPM read.

walk	pull	hold	slide	run	jump	6
dig	hop	play	do	see	step	12
ring	eat	stop	go	climb	fall	18
sing	come	toss	help	meet	smell	24
talk	chat	sleep	ride	fly	sit	30
walk	pull	hold	slide	run	jump	36
dig	hop	play	do	see	step	42
ring	eat	stop	go	climb	fall	48
sing	come	toss	help	meet	smell	54
talk	chat	sleep	ride	fly	sit	60
walk	pull	hold	slide	run	jump	66
dig	hop	play	do	see	step	72
ring	eat	stop	go	climb	fall	78
sing	come	toss	help	meet	smell	84
talk	chat	sleep	ride	fly	sit	90

Total Words Read: _____
Minus errors: _____
= WPM   _____

*Practice these words until you know them!

Name: _____ Date: _____

Fluency Practice – Things

This is a 60 second timed practice. When time is up calculate the total WPM read.

book	tree	log	car	train	tool	6
game	name	cake	sand	door	face	12
nose	bell	note	boat	ship	bike	18
land	baby	bat	can	dish	mat	24
pet	cat	dog	fish	bird	mouse	30
book	tree	log	car	train	tool	36
game	name	cake	sand	door	face	42
nose	bell	note	boat	ship	bike	48
land	baby	bat	can	dish	mat	54
pet	cat	dog	fish	bird	mouse	60
pet	cat	dog	fish	bird	mouse	66
book	tree	log	car	train	tool	72
game	name	cake	sand	door	face	78
nose	bell	note	boat	ship	bike	84
land	baby	bat	can	dish	mat	90
pet	cat	dog	fish	bird	mouse	96
book	tree	log	car	train	tool	102
game	name	cake	sand	door	face	108

Total Words Read: _____
Minus errors: _____
= WPM   _____

Name: _____ Date: _____

Fluency Practice – D, F and G Words

This is a 60 second timed practice. When time is up calculate the total WPM read.

did	dog	duck	do	dull	dot	6
fat	fill	fame	fall	felt	fox	12
gate	go	gum	get	gone	gal	18
door	dip	drip	dad	don't	day	24
fish	for	fun	fit	fog	frog	30
gift	got	give	great	goat	girl	36
did	dog	duck	do	dull	dot	42
fat	fill	fame	fall	felt	fox	48
gate	go	gum	get	gone	gal	54
door	dip	drip	dad	don't	day	60
fish	for	fun	fit	fog	frog	66
gift	got	give	great	goat	girl	72
did	dog	duck	do	dull	dot	78
fat	fill	fame	fall	felt	fox	84
gate	go	gum	get	gone	gal	90
door	dip	drip	dad	don't	day	96
fish	for	fun	fit	fog	frog	102
gift	got	give	great	goat	girl	108

Total Words Read: _____
Minus errors: _____
= WPM _____

Words to Read and Know

Name: _____ Date: _____

Fluency First Hundred – Part 1 Never Enough Practice

This is a 60 second timed practice. When time is up calculate the total WPM read.

the	of	and	a	to	in	6
is	you	that	it	he	was	12
for	on	are	as	with	his	18
they	I	at	be	this	have	24
from	or	one	not	what	all	30
the	of	and	a	to	in	36
is	you	that	it	he	was	42
for	on	are	as	with	his	48
they	I	at	be	this	have	54
from	or	one	not	what	all	60
the	of	and	a	to	in	66
is	you	that	it	he	was	72
for	on	are	as	with	his	78
they	I	at	be	this	have	84
from	or	one	not	what	all	90

Total Words Read: _____
Minus errors: _____
= WPM   _____

Name: _____ Date: _____

Fluency First Hundred – Part 2 Never Enough Practice

This is a 60 second timed practice. When time is up calculate the total WPM read.

were	we	when	you	can	said	6
there	use	an	each	which	she	12
do	how	there	if	will	up	18
other	about	out	many	then	them	24
these	so	some	her	would	make	30
were	we	when	you	can	said	36
there	use	an	each	which	she	42
do	how	there	if	will	up	48
other	about	out	many	then	them	54
these	so	some	her	would	make	60
were	we	when	you	can	said	66
there	use	an	each	which	she	72
do	how	there	if	will	up	78
other	about	out	many	then	them	84
these	so	some	her	would	make	90

Total Words Read: _____
Minus errors: _____
= WPM   _____

Name: _____ Date: _____

Fluency First Hundred – Part 3 Never Enough Practice

This is a 60 second timed practice. When time is up calculate the total WPM read.

like	him	into	time	has	look	6
two	more	write	to	see	number	12
no	way	could	people	my	than	18
first	water	been	called	who	oil	24
sit	now	find	long	down	day	30
like	him	into	time	has	look	36
two	more	write	to	see	number	42
no	way	could	people	my	than	48
first	water	been	called	who	oil	54
sit	now	find	long	down	day	60
like	him	into	time	has	look	66
two	more	write	to	see	number	72
no	way	could	people	my	than	78
first	water	been	called	who	oil	84
sit	now	find	long	down	day	90

Total Words Read: _____
Minus errors: _____
= WPM   _____

Vowels

Name: _____ Date: _____

Fluency – Short Vowels "a"

This is a 60 second timed practice. When time is up calculate the total WPM read.

act	bat	bad	bag	cat	cab	6
dad	fan	fad	had	hat	jam	12
lab	lap	man	mad	nap	pad	18
pal	ran	rag	sad	sat	tab	24
tan	van	gas	mask	past	zap	30
act	bat	bad	bag	cat	cab	36
dad	fan	fad	had	hat	jam	42
lab	lap	man	mad	nap	pad	48
pal	ran	rag	sad	sat	tab	54
act	bat	bad	bag	cat	cab	60
dad	fan	fad	had	hat	jam	66
lab	lap	man	mad	nap	pad	72
pal	ran	rag	sad	sat	tab	78
tan	van	gas	mask	past	zap	84
act	bat	bad	bag	cat	cab	90
dad	fan	fad	had	hat	jam	96

Total Words Read: _____
Minus errors: _____
= WPM _____

Name: _____ Date: _____

Fluency – Short "a"

This is a **one minute** timed reading. When time is up calculate the total CWPM read by using the formula at the bottom of the page.

A bat and a cat were friends. All day long the bat would	13
nap near a rag in the barn. All day long the cat would nap	27
on his man's lap. The bat would nap and the cat would nap.	40
At night the bat and the cat would chase rats. One	51
night, the bad did not feel like chasing rats. One night, the	63
bat decided he would rather pal around with other bats.	73
The cat was very sad. His friend no longer wanted to nap all	86
day. His friend no longer wanted to hunt rats all night.	97
So the cat just sat on his old pal's rag. He was sad and	111
mad. The bat did not mean to make the cat sad. He invited	125
the cat to play with him and other bats. They did not chase	138
rats. Instead, they ran after cabs.	144

Total Words Read: _____
Minus errors: _____
= WPM   _____

Note: Mark the last word read when time is up, but let student finish reading the passage.

Name: _____ Date: _____

Fluency Short Vowel – "e"

This is a 60 second timed practice. When time is up calculate the total WPM read.

bed	beg	dent	fed	gem	get	6
gel	hen	hem	led	let	men	12
met	net	pen	peg	red	set	18
ten	vet	wed	wet	next	neck	24
went	sent	spent	rent	pent	fence	30
bed	beg	dent	fed	gem	get	36
gel	hen	hem	led	let	men	42
met	net	pen	peg	red	set	48
ten	vet	wed	wet	next	neck	54
bed	beg	dent	fed	gem	get	60
gel	hen	hem	led	let	men	66
met	net	pen	peg	red	set	72
ten	vet	wed	wet	next	neck	78
bed	beg	dent	fed	gem	get	84
gel	hen	hem	led	let	men	90
met	net	pen	peg	red	set	96
ten	vet	wed	wet	next	neck	102

Total Words Read: _____
Minus errors: _____
= WPM _____

Name: _____ Date: _____

Fluency – Short "e"

This is a **one minute** timed reading. When time is up calculate the total CWPM read by using the formula at the bottom of the page.

A hen lived in a pen. The pen was ten feet from the	13
barn door. This was a special hen. She was a prize winner.	25
She lived in the pen so the men who owned her could care	38
for her. She lived in the pen so the men could get her ready	52
for the fair.	55
All of the other hens lived outside the fence of her pen.	67
They were free to do what they wanted. They could get food	79
when they wanted. They could play with the other animals	89
when they wanted. The hen wanted out.	96
The hen begged her friend the cow to dent the fence. The	108
hen thought if there was a dent in the fence she would be	121
able to get out. The cow tried to dent the fence. He hurt his	135
head and had to go to the vet.	143
The hen was very sad. Then one morning the men took	154
her to the fair. She won first prize. When she got home, the	167
pen was gone. The hen wore her ribbon all around the	178
barnyard and never had to go into the pen again.	188

Total Words Read: _____
Minus errors: _____
= WPM   _____

Name: _____ Date: _____

Fluency Short Vowel – "i"

This is a 60 second timed practice. When time is up calculate the total WPM read.

bin	bid	big	bit	dim	did	6
dig	dip	fin	fig	fit	gig	12
him	his	hid	hit	hip	jig	18
kin	kid	kit	lid	lit	nip	24
pin	pit	rip	sit	win	zip	30
bin	bid	big	bit	dim	did	36
dig	dip	fin	fig	fit	gig	42
him	his	hid	hit	hip	jig	48
kin	kid	kit	lid	lit	nip	54
pin	pit	rip	sit	win	zip	60
bin	bid	big	bit	dim	did	66
dig	dip	fin	fig	fit	gig	72
him	his	hid	hit	hip	jig	78
kin	kid	kit	lid	lit	nip	84
pin	pit	rip	sit	win	zip	90
bin	bid	big	bit	dim	did	96
dig	dip	fin	fig	fit	gig	102

Total Words Read: _____
Minus errors: _____
= WPM _____

Name: _____   Date: _____

Fluency – Short "i"

This is a **one minute** timed reading. When time is up calculate the total CWPM read by using the formula at the bottom of the page.

Jim had a big bin in his yard. In the bin were bits of dirt	15
and sand. The dirt and sand were for his new tree. His plan	28
was to dig in the dirt. He needed to dig a hole large enough	42
to plant his new fig tree in.	49
Jim did just that. He got a shovel. He dug a hole. He	62
put his fig tree in the hole. The fig tree fit perfectly. He used	76
the bits of dirt and sand from his bin to cover the roots.	89
Jim watered his fig tree each day. He made sure the dirt	100
was loose. He talked to his tree. The tree grew big and	112
strong.	113
The figs grew big. Jim picked the figs when they were big	125
enough to eat. Jim used the bin to put the picked figs in.	138
Jim made fig jam.	142

Total Words Read: _____
Minus errors: _____
= WPM _____

Name: _____ Date: _____

Fluency Short Vowel – "o"

This is a 60 second timed practice. When time is up calculate the total WPM read.

cop	cod	cot	dog	dot	fog	6
hog	jog	log	lot	mop	nod	12
mom	pot	pod	rod	rot	son	18
ton	tot	top	won	off	ox	24
fox	box	blocks	rocks	socks	blog	30
cop	cod	cot	dog	dot	fog	36
hog	jog	log	lot	mop	nod	42
mom	pot	pod	rod	rot	son	48
ton	tot	top	won	off	ox	54
fox	box	blocks	rocks	socks	blog	60
cop	cod	cot	dog	dot	fog	66
hog	jog	log	lot	mop	nod	72
mom	pot	pod	rod	rot	son	78
ton	tot	top	won	off	ox	84
fox	box	blocks	rocks	socks	blog	90

Total Words Read: _____
Minus errors: _____
= WPM _____

Name: _____   Date: _____

Fluency – Short "o"

This is a **one minute** timed reading. When time is up calculate the total CWPM read by using the formula at the bottom of the page.

A dog and a hog lived on a foggy street. A fox and an ox	15
lived across the street. The dog and the hog liked to jog with	28
the fox and the ox. It was a funny sight to see a dog and a	44
hog and a fox and an ox jogging down the street.	55
They liked to jog to the top of the hill. One day they	68
found a box on top of the hill. They took off the lid. It was	83
full of socks. The socks were smelly! When the dog and the	95
hog and the fox and the ox opened the box, the smell filled	108
the air.	110
A mom and her tot were walking by. They smelled the	121
socks and walked over. They asked the dog and the hog and	133
the fox and the ox what was in the box. They all plugged	146
their noses and opened the box. The mom was happy. They	156
were her lost socks.	160
She took the box. She thanked the dog and the hog and	172
the ox and the fox. Then, she took the socks home and	184
washed them.	186

Total Words Read: _____
Minus errors: _____
= WPM   _____

Name: _____ Date: _____

Fluency Short Vowels – "u"

This is a 60 second timed practice. When time is up calculate the total WPM read.

bun	bum	bus	bud	bug	but	6
cut	cup	dug	fun	gun	gum	12
gut	hum	hug	hut	jug	mug	18
pug	pup	rub	run	rut	sub	24
sum	tug	slug	shrug	mud	sun	30
bun	bum	bus	bud	bug	but	36
cut	cup	dug	fun	gun	gum	42
gut	hum	hug	hut	jug	mug	48
pug	pup	rub	run	rut	sub	54
sum	tug	slug	shrug	mud	sun	60
bun	bum	bus	bud	bug	but	66
cut	cup	dug	fun	gun	gum	72
gut	hum	hug	hut	jug	mug	78
pug	pup	rub	run	rut	sub	84
sum	tug	slug	shrug	mud	sun	90

Total Words Read: _____
Minus errors: _____
= WPM _____

Name: _____   Date: _____

Fluency – Short "u"

This is a **one minute** timed reading.

A slug and a bug were friends. They lived in a mug in a	14
bus shed. The bug and the slug liked to go on the buses	27
and chew the used gum.	32
One day a bus driver brought his pug pup to the bus	44
shed. The pug pup and the slug became fast friends. The	55
slug did not like the pup because the pup would run in	67
the yard. He dug in the dirt. He brought dirt into the	79
buses. The slug really did not like a dirty bus.	89
The bug could not understand why the slug did not like	100
the pug. He asked the slug, but the slug would not tell	112
him. The slug just shrugged and moved to sit in the sun.	124
One day the bug saw the slug trying to clean the dirt.	136
He figured out why his bud did not like the pup. He	148
helped clean an old tub. He made sure the pup washed	159
before he came into the bus shed.	166
It worked. Now all three buds have fun chewing the	176
used gum. The slug and the bug and the pug lived happily	188
ever after.	190

Total Words Read: _____
Minus errors: _____
= WPM   _____

Name: _____ Date: _____

Fluency Long Vowels "a"

This is a 60 second timed practice. When time is up calculate the total WPM read.

gate	take	cake	sake	tale	game	6
same	base	late	lake	name	shame	12
baby	paper	lady	case	plane	safe	18
trade	lane	wage	grade	made	date	24
fate	rate	chase	cave	cape	tape	30
gate	take	cake	sake	tale	game	36
same	base	late	lake	name	shame	42
baby	paper	lady	case	plane	safe	48
trade	lane	wage	grade	made	date	54
fate	rate	chase	cave	cape	tape	60
gate	take	cake	sake	tale	game	66
same	base	late	lake	name	shame	72
baby	paper	lady	case	plane	safe	78
trade	lane	wage	grade	made	date	84
fate	rate	chase	cave	cape	tape	90

Total Words Read: _____
Minus errors: _____
= WPM   _____

Name: _____ Date: _____

Fluency – Long "a"

This is a **one minute** timed reading. When time is up calculate the total CWPM read by using the formula at the bottom of the page.

A lady and her baby lived behind a gate. Behind her	11
house was a lake. She kept the gate closed to keep her	23
baby safe. The gate was made out of purple tape! It was a	36
silly gate, but the lady would not trade her gate for even	48
the tastiest cake. She loved her gate.	55
Her baby's name was Nate. When he was old enough	65
he liked to play games by the lake. He made a cave near	78
the lake. He and his friends used the cave as a base for	91
all of their games.	95
The lady was happy Nate liked the lake. The lady was	106
happy his friends liked the lake. She made a cake to	117
celebrate the lake.	120
"It is funny to celebrate a lake," thought Nate. But he	131
ate the cake right up.	136

Total Words Read: _____
Minus errors: _____
= WPM _____

Name: _____ Date: _____

Fluency -- Long "e" Words

This is a 60 second timed practice. When time is up calculate the total WPM read.

me	see	feet	heat	eat	seat	6
he	she	tree	we	me	be	12
keep	steep	sleep	deep	sheep	mean	18
seen	bean	free	tea	pea	sea	24
flea	leaf	green	dream	steam	even	30
me	see	feet	heat	eat	seat	36
he	she	tree	we	me	be	42
keep	steep	sleep	deep	sheep	mean	48
seen	bean	free	tea	pea	sea	54
flea	leaf	green	dream	steam	even	60
me	see	feet	heat	eat	seat	66
he	she	tree	we	me	be	72
keep	steep	sleep	deep	sheep	mean	78
seen	bean	free	tea	pea	sea	84
flea	leaf	green	dream	steam	even	90

Total Words Read: _____
Minus errors: _____
= WPM _____

Name: _____ Date: _____

Fluency – Long "e"

This is a **one minute** timed reading. When time is up calculate the total CWPM read by using the formula at the bottom of the page.

In the park there was a tree. In the tree there lived a	13
flea. He lived on a green leaf. All day the flea dreamed of	26
leaving the tree and sailing out to sea. The only thing was	38
fleas can not swim. This meant that going out to sea would	50
be dangerous.	52
One day while the flea was in a deep sleep, he fell from	65
the tree. He landed on the back of a sheep. It was a mean	79
sheep. The mean sheep tried to pick the flea off. The flea	91
tried to get free from the sheep's back.	99
A bee happened by and saw the flea trying to untangle	110
from the sheep's wool. Being a friendly bee, she distracted	120
the sheep and the flea got away.	127
The flea decided he missed his tree. He forgot his dream	138
of the sea, went back to his tree and lived happily.	149

Total Words Read: _____
Minus errors: _____
= WPM _____

Name: _____ Date: _____

Fluency – Long "i"

This is a 60 second timed practice. When time is up calculate the total WPM read.

kite	bite	right	fight	might	slight	6
side	tide	ride	hide	stride	glide	12
lime	time	chime	mine	fine	sign	18
fire	five	dice	mice	rice	slice	24
ice	iron	bike	like	idea	dive	30
kite	bite	right	fight	might	slight	36
side	tide	ride	hide	stride	glide	42
lime	time	chime	mine	fine	sign	48
fire	five	dice	mice	rice	slice	54
ice	iron	bike	like	idea	dive	60

Total Words Read: _____
Minus errors: _____
= WPM   _____

*Practice these words until you know them!

Name: _____ Date: _____

Fluency – Long "i"

This is a **one minute** timed reading. When time is up calculate the total CWPM read by using the formula at the bottom of the page.

Once upon a time there were three blind mice. Everyday	10
after their noon meal of rice they took turns flying kites.	21
There were three mice but only two kites. The mice were	32
fine with only two kites. They learned to share and to use	44
the word 'ours' instead of 'mine'.	50
One day a slight wind turned to great gusts. One of the	62
mice got caught in the string. The kite took him up and he	75
was gliding over the city.	80
At first, he was frightened, but the longer his ride the	91
braver he got. He liked the wind in his face. He liked gliding	103
over the city.	107
When he got tired, he wanted to get down. He decided to	119
bite a slice in the string. It worked. He thumped down on	131
the ground just in time for dinner.	138

Total Words Read: _____
Minus errors: _____
= WPM _____

Note: Mark the spot when time is up, but let student finish reading the passage.

Name: _____ Date: _____

Fluency -- Long "o" Words

This is a 60 second timed practice. When time is up calculate the total WPM read.

hope	boat	note	moan	foam	mope	6
tow	toad	soak	load	lone	no	12
go	bow	nope	pole	coal	quote	18
roam	toe	so	tone	vote	low	24
bow	bone	rose	oat	zone	phone	30
hope	boat	note	moan	foam	mope	36
tow	toad	soak	load	lone	no	42
go	bow	nope	pole	coal	quote	48
roam	toe	so	tone	vote	low	54
bow	bone	rose	oat	zone	phone	60

Total Words Read: _____
Minus errors: _____
= WPM   _____

*Practice these words until you know them!

Name: _____   Date: _____

Fluency – Long "o"

This is a **one minute** timed reading. When time is up calculate the total CWPM read by using the formula at the bottom of the page.

Joe was in charge of cleaning the mote that surrounded	10
the Castle of Goat. Every day Joe would get in his boat,	22
circle the mote and clean up the garbage.	30
Joe was friends with all of the toads in the mote. Every	42
day he fed them oats and skimmed the foam off of the	54
water so it was fresh and clean.	61
One day Joe got a note from King Goat. King Goat	72
wanted to fill the mote and plant roses. Joe knew if King	84
Goat did this the toads would have no home.	93
Joe told the king he was worried about the toads.	103
"I understand," said the Goat King. "But my wife Flo	113
loves flowers."	115
"I understand too," said Joe. "But you can plant roses	125
in the garden instead. We can use the mote foam to help	137
them grow big and strong."	142
The king thought this was a great idea. It got his vote,	154
and the toads got to keep their home and Flo got the roses	167
she wanted after all.	171

Total Words Read: _____
Minus errors: _____
= WPM   _____

Note: Mark the spot when time is up, but let student finish reading the passage.

Name: _____ Date: _____

Fluency – Long "u" Words

This is a 60 second timed practice. When time is up calculate the total WPM read.

cube	tube	music	cute	flute	mule	6
use	fuse	huge	tulip	suit	juice	12
glue	rule	Ruler	argue	rule	true	18
flu	fruit	suit	fuel	June	tune	24
cube	tube	music	cute	flute	mule	30
use	fuse	huge	tulip	suit	juice	36
glue	rule	ruler	argue	rule	true	42
flu	fruit	suit	fuel	June	tune	48
cube	tube	music	cute	flute	mule	54
use	fuse	huge	tulip	suit	juice	60

Total Words Read: _____
Minus errors: _____
= WPM   _____

*Practice these words until you know them!

Name: _____   Date: _____

Fluency – Long "u"

This is a **one minute** timed reading. When time is up calculate the total CWPM read by using the formula at the bottom of the page.

Last June a mule stopped by my school. He was a	11
friendly mule who knew all of the rules. He was as cute as	24
could be. He was a true, blue friend.	32
When we went into class, Mrs. Jones looked at the mule	43
from over her glasses.	47
"I see we have a new student," Mrs. Jones said.	57
The mule could not speak, so I did it for him.	68
"Yes," I said, "he is used to school and can sit by me."	81
"Very well," Mrs. Jones said.	86
The mule had trouble that day. He couldn't pick up his	97
ruler, he couldn't drink his juice and he couldn't carry a	108
tune during music class.	112
After class, Mrs. Jones said that perhaps the mule would	122
make a better pet than a student.	129
Hummmm, I thought, I wonder what my mom will say?	139

Total Words Read: _____
Minus errors: _____
= WPM   _____

Note: Mark the spot when time is up, but let student finish reading the passage.

Passages

Name: _____ Date: _____

Fluency

This is a **one minute** timed reading. When time is up calculate the total CWPM read by using the formula at the bottom of the page.

There was a boy who did not eat healthy. His name was	12
Jack. He only liked to eat candy. His mom told him he	24
needed to eat better. His dad told him he needed to eat	36
better. His teacher even told him he needed to eat better.	47
Everyday, his mom packed Jack a healthy lunch.	55
Everyday, he traded it for candy and cake. His friend	65
Beth loved his mom's food. She was always willing to trade.	76
His friend Jacob loved his mom's food. He was always	86
willing to trade.	89
One day, Jack went to the dentist. He had two cavities.	100
These were his first cavities. He did not like having cavities.	111
His dentist told him he needed to eat snacks that were	122
better for his teeth. So he did.	129

Total Words Read: _____
Minus errors: _____
= WPM   _____

1. Write one sentence explaining the main topic of the reading:

_____

_____

_____

Name: _____ Date: _____

Comprehension Questions

Please read the questions below and circle the best answer.

1. Jack doesn't eat what kind of food?
    a. good
    b. healthy
    c. sweet
    d. salty

2. Jack only liked to eat:
    a. chocolate
    b. ice cream
    c. carrots
    d. candy

3. Everyday Jack's mother packed him what kind of lunch?
    a. healthy
    b. unhealthy
    c. large
    d. perfect

4. Jack traded his lunches for:
    a. game cards
    b. bubble gum
    c. candy and cake
    d. candy and cupcake

5. Why is Jack eating better?
    a. his mom is making him
    b. his dad said he had to
    c. he got two cavities
    d. his dentist is making him

Name: _____ Date: _____

Fluency – Roots, Stems and Leaves

This is a **one minute** timed reading. When time is up calculate the total CWPM read by using the formula at the bottom of the page.

Water and light are important for plants. Plants use	09
their roots, stems and leaves to get water and light.	19
The stem holds plants up. It also carries water. The	29
leaves use light to make food. Roots keep the plant in the	41
ground. Roots take water from the soil.	48
Plants growing in places where there is little sunlight	57
have large leaves. These leaves help plants get the sun they	68
need. Plants growing in hot places, like the desert, have few	79
leaves. Some plants have no leaves. These no leaf plants	89
store water in their stems.	94

Total Words Read: _____
Minus errors: _____
= WPM _____

1. Write one sentence explaining the main topic of the reading:

_____

_____

_____

Name: _____ Date: _____

Comprehension Questions

Please read the questions below and circle the best answer.

1. What is important for plants?
    a. water and soil
    b. water and air
    c. water and sand
    d. water and light

2. How do plants get water and light?
    e. through their roots and stems
    f. through their roots, stems and leaves
    g. by people watering them
    h. through their leaves

3. What holds plants up
    a. roots
    b. leaves
    c. stems
    d. water

4. Plants growing in places with little sunlight have what kind of leaves?
    a. colorful
    b. large
    c. small
    d. wet

5. Where do no leaf plants store their water?
    a. stem
    b. roots
    c. leaves
    d. flowers

Name: _____ Date: _____

Fluency – What do Flowers Do?

This is a **one minute** timed reading. When time is up calculate the total CWPM read by using the formula at the bottom of the page.

Flowers are the part of the plant that make seeds. Pollen	11
is a powder found inside flowers. It is sticky and tastes good	23
to bees. Flowers use pollen to help make seeds. Bees help to	35
carry pollen from flower to flower so that fruit can grow.	46
Some plants that have flowers make fruit. Seeds form	55
inside the fruit. The fruit keeps the seeds safe.	64
Think about an apple. After you eat it you are left with	76
the core. Think about the little brown seeds inside the core.	87
You can use them to grow apples.	94
Can you name some other seeds you see when you eat	105
fruit?	106

Total Words Read: _____
Minus errors: _____
= WPM   _____

1. Write one sentence explaining the main topic of the reading:

_____

_____

_____

Name: _____ Date: _____

Comprehension Questions

Please read the questions and answer using complete sentences.

1. What part of the plant makes seeds? _____
_____
_____

2. What is pollen used for? _____
_____
_____

3. How does fruit help seeds? _____
_____
_____

4. What is inside of an apple core? _____
_____
_____

5. What can you use seeds for? _____
_____
_____

Name: _____ Date: _____

Fluency – Plant Roots

This is a **one minute** timed reading. When time is up calculate the total CWPM read by using the formula at the bottom of the page.

Plant roots are different from tree to tree. Some roots are	11
thin. Some roots are long. Plants in dry places have long	22
and thin roots. They grow long and thin because they have	33
to find water.	36
Some roots are above the ground. That is because the	46
plants are growing in wet places. They are above the ground	57
so plants do not get too much water.	65
Roots help plants, but they also help animals. Many	74
animals eat roots. These animals depend on roots for their	84
survival.	85
We eat roots, too. A carrot is a root. A beet is a root?	99
What other kinds of roots do you eat?	107

Total Words Read: _____
Minus errors: _____
= WPM   _____

1. Write one sentence explaining the main topic of the reading:

_____

_____

_____

Name: _____ Date: _____

Comprehension Questions

Please read the questions and answer using complete sentences.

1. How are plant roots different from tree to tree? _____
   _____
   _____

2. Why are some roots above the ground? _____
   _____
   _____

3. How do roots help animals? _____
   _____
   _____

4. According to the passage, what kinds of roots do we eat? _____
   _____
   _____

5. Why are some roots long and thin? _____
   _____
   _____

Name: _____ Date: _____

Fluency – Life Cycle

This is a **one minute** timed reading. When time is up calculate the total CWPM read by using the formula at the bottom of the page.

All living things grow, change and make new things. This	10
is called the life cycle. For plants, the life cycle begins with a	23
seed.	24
For pine trees the life cycle begins when the seed forms	35
inside of pine cones. The pine cone seeds are formed. The	46
pine cones fall to the ground. Some seeds stay where they	57
are. Other seeds get carried to new places. A seed becomes	68
a plant. When the plant grows it will grow pine cones of its	81
own.	82
All plants have the same life cycle as their parent plants.	93
Different plants have different life cycles. Some plants live	102
only a few weeks. Other plants live for many, many years.	113

Total Words Read: _____
Minus errors: _____
= WPM _____

1. Write one sentence explaining the main topic of the reading:

_____

_____

_____

Name: _____ Date: _____

Comprehension Questions

Please read the questions and answer using complete sentences.

1. What do all living things do? _____
_____
_____

2. When does the life cycle begin for plants? _____
_____
_____

3. When does the life cyle begin for pine trees? _____
_____
_____

4. All plants have the same life cycle as what? _____
_____
_____

5. Describe the life cycle of a pine tree? _____
_____
_____

Name: _____   Date: _____

Fluency –Soil

This is a **one minute** timed reading. When time is up calculate the total CWPM read by using the formula at the bottom of the page.

Tiny bits of rocks and plants and animals make up soil.	11
Large rocks are broken down by the weather. The large	21
rocks are broken down by water. The large rocks are broken	32
down by wind. The large rocks turn to smaller rocks. The	43
smaller rocks become part of the soil. This is how soil is	55
formed.	56
When plants die, they become part of the soil. When	66
animals die, they become part of the soil.	74
Soil is where most plants grow. Plants use the minerals	84
in the soil to grow big and strong. We use plants to get the	98
minerals we need. This means, that the soil provides us	108
with minerals too.	111

Total Words Read: _____
Minus errors: _____
= WPM   _____

1. Write one sentence explaining the main topic of the reading:

_____

_____

_____

Name: _____ Date: _____

Comprehension Questions

Please read the questions and answer using complete sentences.

1. What makes up soil? _____
_____
_____

2. What are large rocks broken down by? _____
_____
_____

3. What happens to plants when they die? _____
_____
_____

4. What happens to animals when they die? _____
_____
_____

5. Describe how soil is formed? _____
_____
_____

Name: _____ Date: _____

Fluency – The American Badger

This is a **one minute** timed reading. When time is up calculate the total CWPM read by using the formula at the bottom of the page.

American badgers live in the United States. They also	09
live in Canada. They live on the prairie and in farmlands.	21
They are **predators**. This means they hunt and eat other	31
animals to stay alive. They do not eat vegetables or grasses.	42
They only eat meat.	46
They are great at hunting. They are great at digging out	58
their animal prey. They dig out squirrels and other animals.	68
They have long claws to dig with. They can also dig fast.	80
American badgers have short and wide bodies. They	88
have black and white faces. Their coats are gray or brown	99
with white mixed in. Their fur is also coarse.	108

Total Words Read: _____
Minus errors: _____
= WPM _____

1. Write one sentence explaining the main topic of the reading:

_____

_____

_____

Name: _____ Date: _____

Comprehension Questions

Please read the questions and answer using complete sentences.

1. Where do American Badgers live? _____

_____

_____

2. What colors are American Badgers? _____

_____

_____

3. What do American Badgers eat? _____

_____

_____

4. What do they dig with? _____

_____

_____

5. Summarize the passage in two sentences. _____

_____

_____

Name: _____ Date: _____

Fluency – The Arctic Fox

This is a **one minute** timed reading. When time is up calculate the total CWPM read by using the formula at the bottom of the page.

The Arctic fox lives in Alaska. The Arctic fox has fur	11
that changes color. The fur is white in the winter. The fur	23
is brownish-gray in the summer. Its fur changes colors so it	35
can hide in the snow or the dirt.	43
The Arctic fox lives where it is very cold. It fact, its body	56
is made to live in the cold. It is small and low to the ground.	71
Plus, it has a great winter coat. Each October, the Arctic	82
fox's coat thickens. New hairs grow. These hairs are lighter	92
in color than its summer coat. Sadly, this little animal is	103
hunted for this beautiful coat.	108

Total Words Read: _____
Minus errors: _____
= WPM _____

1. Write one sentence explaining the main topic of the reading:

_____

_____

_____

Name: _____ Date: _____

Comprehension Questions

Please read the questions and answer using complete sentences.

1. Where does the Artic fox live? _____

_____

_____

2. What part of the Artic fox changes color? _____

_____

_____

3. Where are their bodies made to live? _____

_____

_____

4. Why is this animal hunted? _____

_____

_____

5. Summarize the passage in two sentences. _____

_____

_____

Name: _____ Date: _____

Fluency – The Giant Panda

This is a **one minute** timed reading. When time is up calculate the total CWPM read by using the formula at the bottom of the page.

Giant pandas are bears. For a time, people thought they	10
were related to raccoons. Scientists have studied them and	19
now we know they are bears.	25
Giant pandas eat mostly bamboo plants. Sometimes	32
they spend 12 hours per day chomping away at bamboo. It	43
eats both the stems and the leaves.	50
The giant panda is **endangered**. There are only about	59
1,000 left in the wild. This means they are protected and	70
can not be hunted.	74
Panda's are black and white. They have white heads.	83
They have black fir around their eyes and on their ears.	94
They live in Central China.	99

Total Words Read: _____
Minus errors: _____
= WPM _____

1. Write one sentence explaining the main topic of the reading:

_____

_____

_____

Name: _____ Date: _____

Comprehension Questions

Please read the questions and answer using complete sentences.

1. What type of animals are giant pandas? _____
_____
_____

2. What do giant pandas eat? _____
_____
_____

3. Why are giant pandas protected? _____
_____
_____

4. Where do giant pandas live? _____
_____
_____

5. Summarize the passage in two sentences. _____
_____
_____

Name: _____ Date: _____

Fluency – Sam's Story

This is a **one minute** timed reading. When time is up calculate the total CWPM read by using the formula at the bottom of the page.

Once there was a boy named Sam. Sam was a small boy	12
for his class. Some of the other kids teased Sam. They	23
called him shrimp. They made him feel bad.	31
Sam felt so bad that one day he decided he didn't want to	44
go to school. He told his mother he was sick. His plan was	57
to be sick forever. He never wanted to go back to school	69
again.	70
That worked for the first day. On the second day, Sam	81
missed his friends. His mom told him that he needed to go	93
to school. Sam decided to tell her what was wrong.	103
They went to school together and told his teacher. The	113
teacher made sure that it never happened in her class again.	124
Sam also told his friend. His friend made sure to stick up	136
for him on the playground and around school.	144

Total Words Read: _____
Minus errors: _____
= WPM _____

1. Write one sentence explaining the main topic of the reading:

_____
_____
_____

Name: _____ Date: _____

Comprehension Questions

Please read the questions and answer using complete sentences.

1. Why did the other kids tease Sam? _____
_____
_____

2. Why did Sam decide he didn't want to go to school? _____
_____
_____

3. What did Sam's mom do to help him? _____
_____
_____

4. What did Sam's friend do? _____
_____
_____

5. Summarize the passage in two sentences. _____
_____
_____

Name: _____ Date: _____

Fluency – Archery

This is a **one minute** timed reading. When time is up calculate the total CWPM read by using the formula at the bottom of the page.

Shooting arrows from bows is called archery. Archery	08
has been around for a long, long time. It has been around	20
since prehistoric times. Arrows were used for battle.	28
Arrows were used to hunt wild animals.	35
Arrows were a tool for survival. Many people still use	45
bows and arrows for hunting. Some countries even still	54
use them as weapons.	58
No one is really sure when the first bows and arrows	69
were used. Today, in the United States, they are used for	80
hunting and for sport. Archery is a target sport. Archers	90
use a longbow to shoot arrows at a target. The target has	102
five colored rings. The smallest ring is in the center. This	113
center ring is called the bull's eye. The archer who hits	124
closest to the bull's eyes gets the most points. The person	135
with the most points at the end of the competition wins.	146

Total Words Read: _____
Minus errors: _____
= WPM   _____

1. Write one sentence explaining the main topic of the reading:

_____

_____

_____

Name: _____ Date: _____

Comprehension Questions

Please read the questions and answer using complete sentences.

1. What is archery? _____
   _____
   _____

2. How long has archery been around? _____
   _____
   _____

3. In the United States bows and arrows are used for what? _____
   _____
   _____

4. What is a bull's eye? _____
   _____
   _____

5. Summarize the passage in two sentences. _____
   _____
   _____

Name: _____   Date: _____

Fluency – Soccer

This is a **one minute** timed reading. When time is up calculate the total CWPM read by using the formula at the bottom of the page.

Soccer is the most popular team sport in the world. It	11
is played on a rectangular field. There is a net goal at both	24
ends of the field. The object of soccer is to get the ball into	38
the other team's goal. The team scoring the most goals	48
wins.	49
There is a catch to playing. Only one person from each	60
team may touch the ball with their hands. This person is	71
called a goalie. He or she guards the goal. Everyone else	83
must use their feet, head or body to move the ball.	94
The rules of soccer are called laws. There are 17 Laws	105
of the Game. Each team may only have eleven players. The	116
world championship of soccer is called the World Cup. It is	127
a world event and is played every four years.	136

Total Words Read: _____
Minus errors: _____
= WPM _____

1. Write one sentence explaining the main topic of the reading:

_____

_____

_____

Name: _____ Date: _____

Comprehension Questions

Please read the questions and answer using complete sentences.

1. What is the most popular sport in the world? _____
_____
_____

2. What is the object of soccer? _____
_____
_____

3. Who may touch the ball with his or her hands? _____
_____
_____

4. How often is the world cup played? _____
_____
_____

5. Summarize the passage in two sentences. _____
_____
_____

Name: _____ Date: _____

Fluency

This is a **one minute** timed reading. When time is up calculate the total CWPM read by using the formula at the bottom of the page.

Jay jumped off the bus and ran straight home. He	10
slammed open the door. He threw his backpack on the	20
hallway floor. He ran to the kitchen. It was there, under the	32
phone. His package from Grandma had arrived.	39
He called for his mother. She raced into the kitchen.	49
Mother helped him open the box. He tore open the bubble	60
wrap. And there it was. A baggie filled with double	70
chocolate chip cookies.	73
His mouth watered. He opened the zipper on the bag.	83
The smell of the cookies made his mouth water more. He	94
took out a cookie. He took a giant bite.	103
He smiled at his mother. Now he had the energy to do	115
his homework.	117

Total Words Read: _____
Minus errors: _____
= WPM _____

1. Write one sentence explaining the main topic of the reading:

_____

_____

_____

Name: _____ Date: _____

Comprehension Questions

Please read the questions and answer using complete sentences.

1. What did Jay do after he jumped off the bus? _____
_____
_____

2. Why did Jay call for his mother? _____
_____
_____

3. What was in the box? _____
_____
_____

4. What did Jay now have the energy to do? _____
_____
_____

5. Summarize the passage in two sentences. _____
_____
_____

Name: _____   Date: _____

Fluency – Penguins 1.9

This is a **one minute** timed reading. When time is up calculate the total CWPM read by using the formula at the bottom of the page.

Penguins are graceful in the water. Their speedy	08
swimming skills make up for the fact that they can't fly.	19
Penguins can't fly, but they are birds. These birds hunt fish.	30
These birds hunt krill and squid, too. They hunt fish in the	42
ocean. In cold months, penguins swim south. In warm	51
months, they move onto land and breed.	58
Emperor penguins are penguins we have all seen. They	67
have sleek bodies and flat wings. Their wings are really their	78
flippers. They use these wings or flippers to cut through the	89
water. Their bodies are covered by feathers. Emperor	97
penguins have a thick layer of blubber to help keep them	108
warm. They need to keep warm because they live in the icy	120
Antarctic waters.	122
Penguins don't always seem like birds, but they are!	131

Total Words Read: _____
Minus errors: _____
= WPM   _____

1. Write one sentence explaining the main topic of the reading:

_____

_____

Name: _____ Date: _____

Comprehension Questions – Penguins

Please read the questions and answer using complete sentences.

1. What type of animal is a penguin? _____
_____
_____

2. What do penguins hunt? _____
_____
_____

3. What do penguins use their wings for? _____
_____
_____

4. Describe an Emperor Penguin? _____
_____
_____

5. Summarize the passage in two sentences. _____
_____
_____

Name: _____ Date: _____

Fluency – Birds of Prey 2.3

This is a **one minute** timed reading. When time is up calculate the total CWPM read by using the formula at the bottom of the page.

Birds of prey are predators. They have large eyes and	10
excellent hearing. Their large eyes and their excellent	18
hearing help to make them great hunters. They also have a	29
super sense of smell. This also helps birds of prey hunt for	41
their food. The smallest birds of prey hunt for insects. The	52
large birds of prey can hunt and kill young deer. These	63
large birds of prey are called raptors. An eagle is a raptor.	75
All raptors have similar features. They all have curved	84
beaks. Their beaks have sharp edges to help them tear apart	95
prey. Raptors also have sharp talons. In fact the talons, or	106
claws, on their feet are deadly and help them kill, hold and	118
carry their prey. Most birds of prey have three toes pointing	129
forward and one pointing back.	134
Raptors lay eggs. When the mother bird is keeping the	144
eggs warm so they can hatch, the father bird goes for food.	156
It takes raptors from 26 to 50 days to hatch their eggs. That	169
is a lot of sitting.	174

Total Words Read: _____
Minus errors: _____
= WPM _____

Name: _____ Date: _____

1. Write one sentence explaining the main topic of the reading:

_____

_____

Comprehension Questions – Birds of Prey

Please read the questions and answer using complete sentences.

1. Describe a bird of prey? _____

_____

_____

2. Describe the features raptors? _____

_____

_____

3. Why do raptors have sharp beaks? _____

_____

_____

4. How long does it take for raptor eggs to hatch? _____

_____

_____

Name: _____   Date: _____

Fluency – Falcon, Vultures and Eagles 2.7

This is a **one minute** timed reading. When time is up calculate the total CWPM read by using the formula at the bottom of the page.

Falcons, vultures and eagles are all birds of prey.	09
The fastest bird of prey is the peregrine falcon. It is	20
between 13 and 20 inches long. It weighs from one to three	32
pounds. It eats small birds. It hunts and swoops down to	43
catch its prey traveling 220 miles per hour.	51
The griffon vulture looks frightening, but it does not kill.	61
It is a scavenger. It feeds on dead animals. Vultures eat the	73
leftovers of other birds. Vultures are about 40 inches tall	83
and weight about 20 pounds.	88
The bald eagle is a bird of prey. It is also a symbol of the	103
United States of America. Bald eagles are about 20 inches	113
long and weigh an average of 11 pounds. Eagles fish for	124
their food. They swoop down and grab fish with their talons.	135

Total Words Read: _____
Minus errors: _____
= WPM _____

1. Write one sentence explaining the main topic of the reading:

_____

_____

Name: _____ Date: _____

Comprehension Questions – Falcons, Vultures and Eagles

Please read the questions and answer using complete sentences.

1. Describe a falcon? _____
   _____
   _____

2. What are the physical features of a vulture? _____
   _____
   _____

3. What do eagles eat? _____
   _____
   _____

4. How are the three birds in the passage different? _____
   _____
   _____

5. Summarize the passage in two sentences. _____
   _____
   _____

173

Name: _____   Date: _____

Fluency – Fish 2.9

This is a **one minute** timed reading. When time is up calculate the total CWPM read by using the formula at the bottom of the page.

Fish are the oldest group of vertebrates on earth. They	10
are also the biggest. They are the first animals to have	21
backbones. Fish breath through their gills. Fish get oxygen	30
using these gills. Water enters their mouths, flows over their	40
gills and out under their gill covers. The gill covers are on	52
the side of the heads of fish.	59
The most feared fish is the great white shark. The great	70
white shark is a predator. They eat large fish, squid and	81
seals. Great white sharks are protected. They are protected	90
because there aren't many of them left in the ocean. People	101
overfished them and now they are endangered.	108
The giant sea bass is not overfished. They swim off of the	120
California coast. They also live in Mexico and Japan. Some	130
giant sea bass are over 100 years old.	138
Fish are fun to look at and some are tasty to eat. What is	152
your favorite kind of fish?	157

Total Words Read: _____
Minus errors: _____
= WPM   _____

Name: _____ Date: _____

1. Write one sentence explaining the main topic of the reading:

_____
_____
_____
_____

Comprehension Questions – Fish

Please read the questions and answer using complete sentences.

1. What are fish the first animals to have? _____

_____
_____

2. How do gills work? _____

_____
_____

3. Describe a great white shark? _____

_____
_____

4. Where do giant sea bass live? _____

_____
_____

Name: _____   Date: _____

Fluency – Bears 1.7

This is a **one minute** timed reading. When time is up calculate the total CWPM read by using the formula at the bottom of the page.

A bear is a mammal. There are only eight species of	11
bears. They all have common characteristics. They have	19
large bodies. They have short, stocky legs. They have long	29
shouts and tangly hair. They have paws with five claws.	39
Their claws do not retract. They have short tales.	48
Some bears are carnivores. A carnivore eats meat. Polar	57
bears eat meat. Some bears only eat plants. Giant pandas	67
have a diet of bamboo. That is all they eat. The other six	70
species of bears are omnivores. That means they eat a	80
mixture of meat and plants.	85
Bears have a keen sense of smell. They are big and look	97
clumsy, but bears run very fast. Most bears stay in their	108
dens and sleep all winter long. Their sleep in called	118
hibernation. Hibernation can last up to 100 days.	126
Bears have been on the earth long than humans. Have	136
you ever seen a bear?	141

Total Words Read: _____
Minus errors: _____
= WPM _____

Name: _____ Date: _____

1. Write one sentence explaining the main topic of the reading:

_____

_____

_____

_____

Comprehension Questions – Fish

Please read the questions and answer using complete sentences.

1. Name two things you learned about bears? _____

_____

_____

2. What do polar bears eat? _____

_____

_____

3. What do giant pandas eat? _____

_____

_____

4. How long can bears hibernate? _____

_____

_____

Story Passages

Peanut and the Plant
Fluency

The following reading selections are from the short story <u>Peanut and the Plant</u>. They are laid out to be read on consecutive days. The passages change from one minute timed readings to two minute timed readings as the story progresses.

To calculate the Combined Words Per Minute for two minute passages:
1. Set the timer for two minutes
2. Mark the last word read after two minutes have passed
3. Let student finish reading
4. Count the total words read (CWPM)
5. Divide the total words read by two

There are no comprehension exercises for this section. The individual passages contain a continuous story, so it is important to discuss what was read the previous day with with your class before you read the new text.

Paired Summaries: There is a summary template following the story fluency passages. An alternate assignment is to have students complete the fluency activity and then write a paired summary paragraph. After all students are finished with their paragraphs, have volunteers share what they wrote.

Have *Early Finisher* assignments on hand for students who complete the assignment before the majority of the class.

Name: _____ Date: _____

Fluency

This is a **two minute** timed reading. When time is up calculate the total CWPM read by using the formula at the bottom of the page.

Peanut jumped the knee-high brick planter between	8
her landing and mine. She called up to my window.	18
Peanut is my best friend. We live in the same house only	30
in different homes. We live in the Mission District of San	40
Francisco.	41
Our house is like a lot of the other houses on our street.	54
It is tall and skinny and divided in half, so two families can	67
live in the same house only with no doors to the other side.	79
I opened the door when I heard her voice. I was already	91
ready. We share a wall. My canary yellow bedroom	100
slapped right up to her girlie pink one.	108
She knocked three times before she left.	115
This is my cue to meet her outside. Three knocks to	126
meet outside. Two knocks to call or text. One to say good	138
night at 8:30 sharp. Today, we are going hunting, nature	148
hunting. Nature hunting in our neighborhood is tough.	156
Some of San Francisco has no wildlife.	163

Total Words Read: _____
Divided by 2: _____
Minus errors: _____
= WPM _____

Name: _____ Date: _____

Fluency

This is a **two minute** timed reading. When time is up calculate the total CWPM read by using the formula at the bottom of the page.

Again, we are going hunting, nature hunting. Nature	08
hunting in our neighborhood is tough. Some of San	17
Francisco does have great wildlife.	22
Flowers and trees and birds and bushes make some	31
places not even seem like a city. On our street it's mostly,	43
house after house, after house, after house, after apartment	52
building, after house…and so on until you hit Mission	62
Street.	63
On our side of Mission is Top's Market. Across the street	74
is a Starbuck's knockoff. Cement and asphalt line the	83
streets with only an occasional tree. We are going to change	94
that. We are going to plant jungly vines in the planter	95
between our front doors.	99

Total Words Read: _____
Minus errors: _____
= WPM   _____

1. Write one sentence explaining the main topic of the reading:

_____

_____

_____

Name: _____ Date: _____

Fluency

This is a **one minute** timed reading. When time is up calculate the total CWPM read by using the formula at the bottom of the page.

We are going to plant jungly vines in the planter between	11
our front doors. They will grow and grow and grow until	22
they overtake the walls and ceilings. They will grow and	32
grow and grow until they hang over the front of the porch.	44
People will have to hack their way inside our houses.	55
"One, two..." I count the lines in the cement.	63
"Three, four, first tree..." Peanut says her part of the	73
counting game we play. "Hey Mickey?" She asks me.	82
"Yea?" I continue skipping along the sidewalk.	89
"Where are we going to get these vines?"	97
I shrug my shoulders as I wave to old Mrs. Beck.	108

Total Words Read: _____
Minus errors: _____
= WPM _____

1. Write one sentence explaining the main topic of the reading:

_____

_____

_____

Name: _____ Date: _____

Fluency

This is a **one minute** timed reading. When time is up calculate the total CWPM read by using the formula at the bottom of the page.

I shrug my shoulders as I wave to old Mrs. Beck.	11
"Hi, Mrs. Beck!" Peanut and I call together.	19
"Hello, girls." She smiles and waves from her porch	28
landing. She is sitting behind an easel.	35
Peanut turns and skips up her walk. I follow.	44
"What're you painting today Mrs. Beck?" Peanut asks as	53
she hops the last step and looks at the easel. "Pretty."	64
"Thank you," Mrs. Beck smiles. When she does, her	73
face scrunches up like one of the fans on the wall at Top's	86
Market. Her face scrunches, but her blue eyes twinkle.	95
"These are the roses I had in my garden when I was a little	109
girl. I'm sure they are much bigger now."	117

Total Words Read: _____
Minus errors: _____
= WPM _____

1. Write one sentence explaining the main topic of the reading:

_____

_____

_____

Name: _____ Date: _____

Fluency

This is a **two minute** timed reading. When time is up calculate the total CWPM read by using the formula at the bottom of the page.

I take my own look. "Pretty, pretty," I say.	9
Mrs. Beck has lived in San Francisco all of her life. She tells us	23
stories about when there were parks all around. When wild animals	34
like raccoons and skunks and rabbits would rummage through her	44
garbage. When there were actually cow pastures here.	52
Imagine. Cow pastures in San Francisco.	58
Think about it...cows wandering the streets of San Francisco and	69
sitting on the cable car lines? That would be a sight.	70
"What are you girls up to today?"	77
"We are going hunting," Peanut states proudly.	84
Mrs. Beck unscrunches her cheeks and puts the scrunch	93
between her eyes. "My, my...and what are you hunting for?"	104
"Wild jungly plants," I state and take deep breath. "We are going	116
to plant jungly vines in the planter between our front doors. They will	129
grow and grow and grow until they overtake the walls and ceilings and	142
hang over the front of the porch and people have to hack their way	156
inside our houses."	159
"I see," she smiles. "Where are you going to get these vines?" Mrs.	172
Beck asks.	174

Total Words Read: _____
Divided by 2: _____
Minus errors: _____
= WPM _____

1. Write one sentence explaining the main topic of the reading:

_____

_____

_____

Name: _____ Date: _____

Fluency

This is a **two minute** timed reading. When time is up calculate the total CWPM read by using the formula at the bottom of the page.

"If we knew that we would not have to hunt for them," Peanut	13
says politely. When Peanut says something like that it comes out	24
politely. Now, if I said it, for some reason, it would not sound so very	39
polite.	40
"There's just not enough nature in our environment," I state.	50
Environment was one of our spelling words. I like to use our spelling	63
words when I talk. It makes me sound smart.	72
"You girls are right there. That's why I like my paintings. I	84
put them on the wall and nature comes inside my house," Mrs. Beck	97
smiles. "Good luck on your hunt."	103
Our first stop is the seed section of Murikami's Market. We spin	115
the seed holder rack.	119
"Peas, carrots, squash, beans..." Peanut reads the packages.	127
Mrs. Murikami calls from behind the counter. "Can I help you	138
girls find something?"	141
I walk over and lean on the counter. I wave to Mr. Murikami	154
who is kneeling under the counter untangling cords. "We're looking	164
for tangly, jungly vines to plant on our front porch."	174

Total Words Read: _____
Divided by 2: _____
Minus errors: _____
= WPM _____

1. Write one sentence explaining the main topic of the reading:

_____

_____

_____

Name: _____ Date: _____

Fluency

This is a **two minute** timed reading. When time is up calculate the total CWPM read by using the formula at the bottom of the page.

"Will these work Mickey?" Mr. Murikami holds up the black	10
and gray cords. "They are about as tangled as it gets."	21
"We want the real kind," Peanut has looked at all of the seed	34
packages and joins me at the counter.	41
I take a deep breath. "We are going to plant jungly vines in the	55
planter between our front doors. They will grow and grow and grow	67
until they overtake the walls and ceilings and hang over the front of	80
the porch and people have to hack their way inside our houses."	92
"I see," Mrs. Murikami said thoughtfully. "I'm sorry girls, we	102
only carry vegetable seeds."	106
"Thanks anyway," I say as the door jingler jingles.	115
We leave disappointed.	118
"Good luck," calls Mr. Murikami.	123
We wave and head towards Pay Hardware. Inside we search the	134
seed rack with the same results...vegetables. Nothing but vegetables.	144
Doesn't anyone plant anything but vegetables in this town?	153
What about plants and flowers? Someone must sell seeds for them or	165
else how would they get them to grow in the park or in the country?	180
They can't just appear. That's just crazy.	187

Total Words Read: _____
Divided by 2: _____
Minus errors: _____
= WPM _____

1. Write one sentence explaining the main topic of the reading:

_____

_____

_____

Name: _____ Date: _____

Fluency

This is a **two minute** timed reading. When time is up calculate the total CWPM read by using the formula at the bottom of the page.

As we are leaving the store I spot it...the most beautiful yellow	13
and green viney plant I have ever seen. It is hanging in a section with	28
other plants.	30
"Eureka!" I say and head straight to it. Eureka is a word from	43
our gold rush lesson in Social Studies. It means 'I found it'. Miners	56
used to say it when they found gold. Well, this jungly vine is my gold,	71
so I figure it is a good place to use the word.	83
"Oh, Mickey, it's perfect. Only it's growing down not up,"	93
Peanut says.	95
We are now standing under the plant. It is perfect. "All we have	108
to do is train it to go up."	116
"Good idea," Peanut says as a man in a red vest approaches.	128
"Can I help you ladies?" He asks.	135
"How much is this plant?" I ask and then I hold my breath.	158
Please be less then $18.24...I say over and over in my head.	171
He looks at the tag...and... "Twelve ninety-nine."	180
"We'll take it," Peanut and I say together.	188
The guy in the red vest rings us up and we head for home.	202

Total Words Read: _____
Divided by 2: _____
Minus errors: _____
= WPM _____

1. Write one sentence explaining the main topic of the reading:

_____

_____

_____

Name: _____   Date: _____

Fluency

This is a **two minute** timed reading. When time is up calculate the total CWPM read by using the formula at the bottom of the page.

We dig up the deep brown dirt in the planter and plop in our	14
beautiful jungly vine. We give our jungly plant plenty of water. The	26
plant looks good there between our front doors. "When it gets junglier	38
we'll staple the vines to the side of the house so it grows up," I say to	55
Peanut.	56
I hope my mom won't mind few staples in the siding.	67
"How long to you think it will take to grow?" Peanut asks.	79
"A few days probably," I say, but I'm really not sure.	89
Every day we water the jungly vine. Every day we talk to the	101
jungly vine. Every day we measure the jungly vine's long shoots.	112
Every day our jungly vine looks sicker and sicker.	121
Standing on our porch Wednesday after school, Peanut says	130
what we have both been thinking. "Mickey, I think our jungly vine is	143
dying."	144
We hear the wheels of Mrs. Beck's walker before we see her	156
coming up the walk. "It's dying because it is a houseplant."	167
I survey my surroundings. Is she crazy? This is a house. "Ah,	179
Mrs. Beck, this is a house."	185
She smiles that crinkle face smile that lights up her eyes. "No,	197
no Mickey, houseplant means that it is an inside plant."	198

Total Words Read: _____
Divided by 2: _____ Minus errors: _____ = WPM _____

1. Write one sentence explaining the main topic of the reading:

_____

_____

_____

Name: _____   Date: _____

Fluency

This is a **two-minute** timed reading. When time is up calculate the total CWPM read by using the formula at the bottom of the page.

"What difference does it make?" Peanut asks.	07
Mrs. Beck explains. "It is warmer inside and not as	17
damp. This is a tropical plant. It needs lots of warm air."	29
"We could cover it at night," I suggest.	37
"It can't die, we spent almost all of our allowance on it,"	49
Peanut sighs.	51
"Try covering it girls, but I don't know how much good	62
it will do." Mrs. Beck begins back down the walk. "Most of	74
the jungly plants you'd be interested in are for tropical	84
climates, meaning that they will not grow in San Francisco."	94
I am so heartbroken that I can only nod. I am	105
heartbroken, but I will not give up hope. Our jungly vine	116
will live. I just know it...	122
Every night for the next two weeks we cover our plant	133
with an old sheet and it works. Our house plant loves its	145
spot on the porch, as long as we tuck it in at night	162

Total Words Read: _____
Divided by 2: _____ Minus errors: _____ = WPM _____

1. Write one sentence explaining the main topic of the reading:

_____

_____

_____

Name: _____ Date: _____

Summary Graphic Organizer

Title: _____

Main Idea:

Circle Three Important Words in the Main Idea and Write Them Here:

_____   _____   _____

Three Important Detail

1. _____
2. _____
3. _____

Summary of the Passage in One Sentence

_____
_____
_____

Inventory Sheets and Logs

Oral Reading Fluency

Reading fluency is basically the speed or rate of reading, as well as the ability to read while expressing smoothly, effortless and automatically without thought to the decoding process.

A student's reading rate is calculated by dividing the number of words read correctly by the total time reading. The drills in this handbook are designed as reads to help build fluency. They are embedded in the activities, take minutes out of the day and work well in an RTI setting or as a whole class activity.

As a general guide, students should reach the following fluency benchmarks:

Grade One

Fall	
Winter	47-85 words per minute
Spring	90-115 words per minute

Grade Two

Fall	79 - 106 words per minute
Winter	100-125 words per minute
Spring	117-142 words per minute

Grade Three

Fall	79 - 110 words per minute
Winter	93 - 123 words per minute
Spring	114 - 142 words per minute

Name: _____ Date: _____

Oral Fluency Record

Passage Number	DATE	CWPM	DATE	CWPM	DATE	CWPM	DATE	CWPM	DATE	CWPM

CWPM = correct words per minute

Name: _____ Date: _____

Oral Fluency Graphs

130																					
125																					
120																					
115																					
110																					
105																					
100																					
95																					
90																					
85																					
80																					
75																					
70																					
65																					
60																					
55																					
50																					
45																					
40																					
35																					
30																					
25																					
20																					
15																					
10																					
5																					
0																					
DATE																					
PASSAGE NUMBER																					

Name: _____ Date: _____

Oral Fluency Graphs

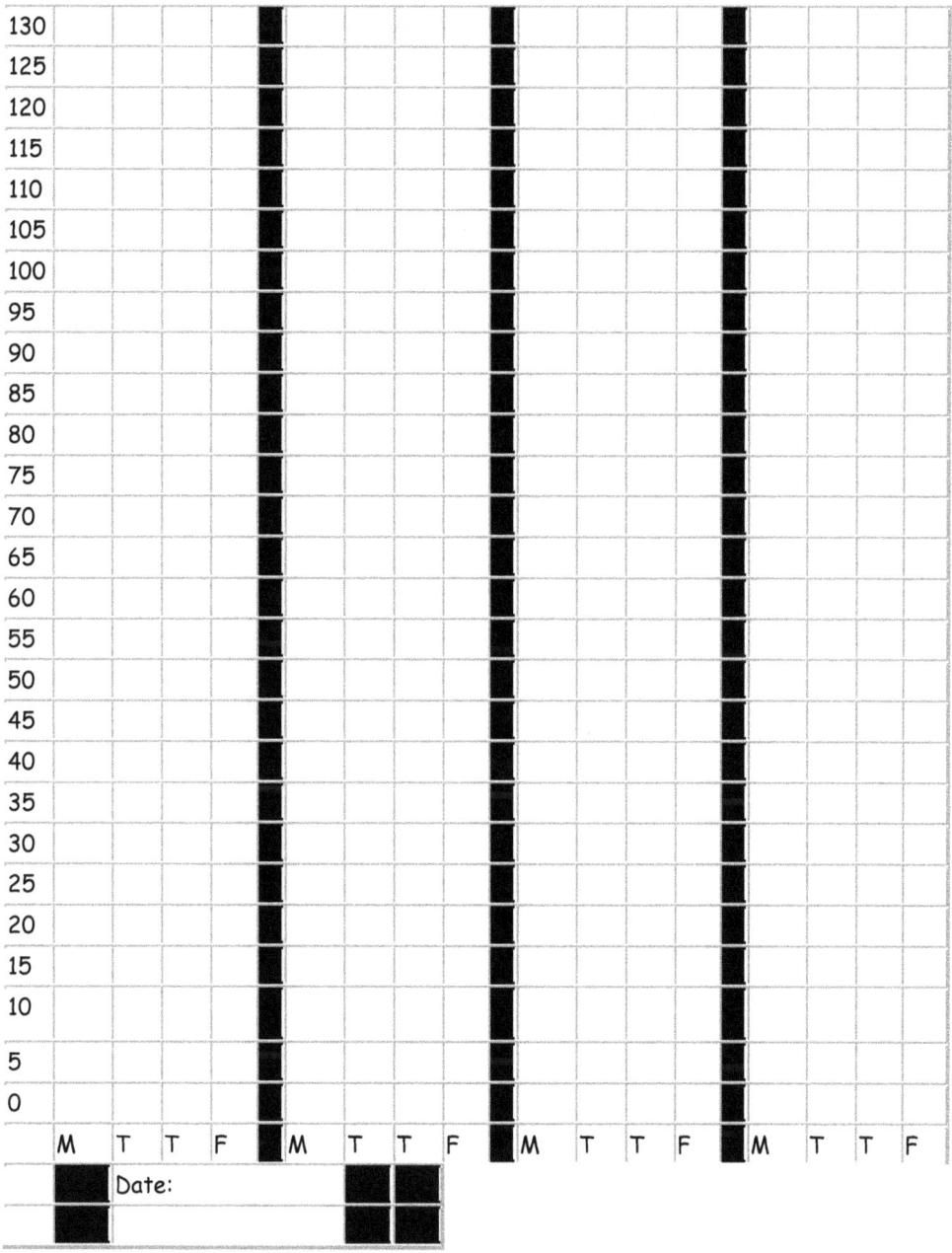

197

Resources

Foorman, B. R., Fletcher, J., & Francis, D. (1997). A scientific approach to reading instruction.

Foorman, B.R., Francis, D.J., Fletcher, J.M., Winikates, D., & Mehta, P. (1997). Early interventions for children with reading problems. Scientific Studies of Reading, 1(3), 255-276. (Special issue on reading interventions)

Foorman, B.R., Francis, D.J, Shaywitz, S.E., Shaywitz, B.A., & Fletcher, J.M. (1997). The case for early reading interventions. In B. Blachman (Ed.), Foundations of reading acquisition and dyslexia: Implications for early intervention (pp. 243-264). Mahwah, NJ: Erlbaum.

Shaywitz, S. E. (2003). Overcoming Dyslexia. Random House Inc., NY.

Please check out www.luckyjenny.com for other curriculum and classroom needs.

www.ingramcontent.com/pod-product-compliance
Lightning Source LLC
Chambersburg PA
CBHW081345040426
42450CB00015B/3311